Igloo Dwellers
Were My Church

John R. Sperry

With a foreword by the
Honourable Jake Ootes, Minister of Education,
Government of the Northwest Territories.

Bayeux

Arts Inc.

Igloo Dwellers Were My Church

© 2001 John R. Sperry and Bayeux Arts, Inc.

Published by: Bayeux Arts, Inc., Calgary, Alberta, Canada

Cover design by: Heidi Held, John Pekelsky
Designed by: JP, Elizabeth Gilbert, Dot Van Vliet,

Outcrop Communications Ltd., Yellowknife,
   Northwest Territories, Canada

Cover photographs: John R. Sperry, Harold Webster,
                   Jiri Hermann, and Alec Algiak

Canadian Cataloguing in Publication Data

Sperry, John R., 1927- Igloo Dwellers Were My Church

1. Sperry, John R.
2. Anglican Church of Canada – Bishops – Biography.
3. Bishops – Canada, Northern.
4. Missionaries – Canada, Northern – Biography.
5. Inuit – Missions – Canada. I. Title.

BX5620.S645A3 2001   283'.092   C2001-910102-3

First Printing: March 2001

Printed in Hong Kong by King's Time Industries.

*The Publisher gratefully acknowledges the financial support of the Canada Council
for the Arts, the Alberta Foundation for the Arts, and the Government of Canada
through the Book Publishing Industry Development Program.*

Table of Contents

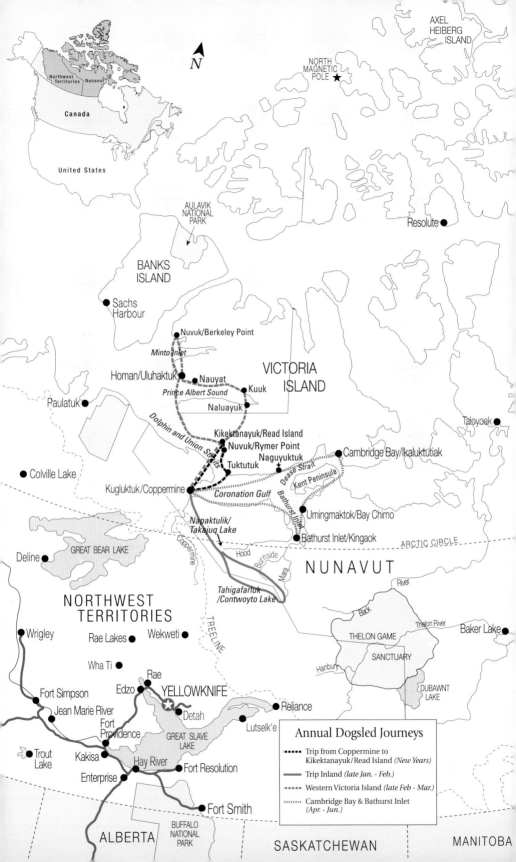

AXEL
HEIBERG
ISLAND

N

NORTH
MAGNETIC
POLE ★

Canada

Northwest
Territories   Nunavut

United States

Resolute ●

AULAVIK
NATIONAL
PARK

BANKS
ISLAND

● Sachs
Harbour

● Nuvuk/Berkeley Point

Minto Inlet

VICTORIA
ISLAND

Homan/Uluhaktuk ●   ● Nauyat

Prince Albert Sound   ● Kuuk

● Paulatuk   Naluayuk

Taloyoak ●

Dolphin and Union Straits

● Kikektanayuk/Read Island

● Colville Lake   Nuvuk/Rymer Point

Naguyuktuk

● Cambridge Bay/Ikaluktutiak

Tuktutuk   *Dease Strait*

Kent Peninsula

Kugluktuk/Coppermine ●   *Coronation Gulf*

Bathurst Inlet

*Napaktulik/
Takaiuq Lake*   Umingmaktok/Bay Chimo ●

● Deline   GREAT BEAR LAKE   *Coppermine*   Bathurst Inlet/Kingaok ●

ARCTIC CIRCLE

Hood   NUNAVUT

Burnside

Maa

*Tahigafarluk
/Contwoyto Lake*   *River*

NORTHWEST
TERRITORIES   *Back*   Thelon River   ● Baker Lake

● Wrigley   Rae Lakes ●   Wekweti ●   TREELINE   THELON GAME
SANCTUARY

Wha Ti ●   *Hanbury*

Rae ●   DUBAWNT
LAKE

Edzo ●   YELLOWKNIFE

● Fort Simpson   ★   ● Detah   ● Reliance

Jean Marie River ●   Lutselk'e ●   **Annual Dogsled Journeys**

Fort
Providence   GREAT SLAVE
LAKE   ••••• Trip from Coppermine to
Kikektanayuk/Read Island *(New Years)*

● Trout
Lake   Kakisa ●   Hay River ●   ● Fort Resolution   ——— Trip Inland *(late Jan. - Feb.)*

Enterprise ●   ------- Western Victoria Island *(late Feb - Mar.)*

● Fort Smith   .... Cambridge Bay & Bathurst Inlet
(Apr. - Jun.)

ALBERTA   BUFFALO
NATIONAL
PARK   SASKATCHEWAN   MANITOBA

Dedication

To my wife, Betty, and our children, Angela and John,
whose love and unfailing support throughout the years recorded
in this book, and ever since, are acknowledged with deep
appreciation and gratitude.

A tribute of thanks to the people of the land....

Uvani makpigagmi uvanga inuhiga, Kugluktumiuniitillunga
unipkautigivaktagaluaga tiitigakhunga kavlunaaktun kihimi.

Atautikun kuyagiyakhagiyatka inuit tamangmik, umatillugit,
tikilihaktillunga talvangaanillu, amihun ikayukpagmannga inuit
pikuhingnik ilitukhikuvlunga inuinaktun inuit tamangmitiak
kangekhikuvlugit Godim Ukauhianik.

Aahin, Kitengmiunun allanun aullagumagagama kenmitigun,
inungnin ikayuktauningnakpaktungali aullaami nangiahukunanga
munagiyauvlungalu ukiuk taman. Ila inuit kuanakpiaktun
tapkunani nayukataugapta, ilatkalu ukiuk 1950minganin
1970munaktumun. Ilaa Godim ilagitigut tamapta.

John R. Sperry

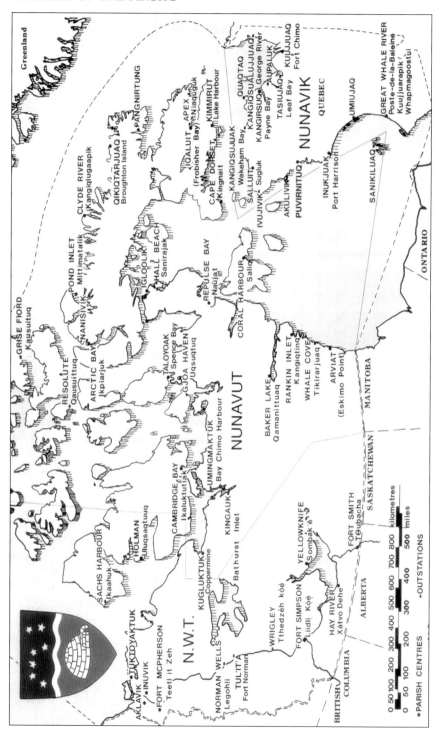

Foreword

Few people would probably have guessed that the young John Sperry, born in Leicester, England in 1924, the son of a hardworking man with a shoemaking business, would play a pivotal role in the development of a remote area in the Canadian Arctic. However, the man who became the third Bishop of the Arctic was not surprised to find himself ministering to the Inuit in the Central Arctic region of the Northwest Territories.

In this record of his noteworthy life, Bishop Sperry tells us how he came to be a minister in the Canadian Arctic and about his life with the Inuit whom he grew to admire and respect.

Bishop Sperry's childhood family was Methodist and Anglican— both traditions in which missionary work played a vital role. He knew from a young age that he wanted to be a missionary in the Canadian Arctic. A series of coincidences, part of what he thinks of as the mysterious ways in which God moves, resulted in his coming to Coppermine (now re-named Kugluktuk) in 1950 as an Anglican missionary.

To minister to his flock, the missionary Sperry first had to learn the complex Inuit language. He became so proficient he was able to translate the Gospels and Acts of the New Testament, and several other documents of the Anglican faith, into Inuinaktun. This allowed the Inuit of the area to worship in their own language for the first time—and earned their appreciation and respect.

John Sperry also quickly learned to live and travel like the Inuit, travelling some 3000 miles by dogteam each winter and by boat in the summer, serving his parishioners in their far-flung camps. He brought them not only the word of God, but also mail, news from other people in the region, medical and rudimentary dental services.

Bishop Sperry's book is not only a record of the traditional ways of life in the Central Arctic in the 1950s and 1960s, but also the per-sonal account of a man who became known for his sensitivity, humility and compassion. He and his wife Elizabeth are still warm-ly loved by the Central Arctic Inuit for their services during the good times of health and plenty, as well as the terrible times of epidemic and famine. The Sperrys are remembered because they did not set themselves apart from the people with whom they lived and worked, and for the respect they had for the traditional beliefs of their Inuit hosts.

This is a fascinating slice of first-hand experience of a unique time in the Northwest Territories, when the Inuit made the transition from living in traditional nomadic groups to life in permanent communities. Told from the viewpoint of a European missionary, this account is a welcome addition to the other voices of this historical period.

I would like to express my gratitude to Bishop Sperry for writing this book, which preserves this extraordinary window of time in the history of the Arctic and its people.

Honourable Jake Ootes
Minister of Education, Culture and Employment
Government of the Northwest Territories

Introduction & Acknowledgements

As I worked at Bathurst Inlet during the summer of the year 2000, I was honoured by satellite phone calls from all over the Arctic, congratulating me on the fiftieth anniversary of my arrival in Coppermine (now called Kugluktuk). I looked out at the stunning scenery of the Inlet, and on the welcoming faces of friends in this small community, and reflected upon how blessed I feel to have been resident in the Arctic, and a part, however small, of the great and never-ending story of Canada's North.

For the last ten years, friends across the North and around the world have been urging me to share the story of the twenty years I spent with my family, parishioners and friends in the central Arctic. Other projects always seemed to intervene, but at last, here it is, with appreciation to all those (including my family) who kept saying, "Get to it!"

I have kept diaries all my life, but my diaries, unfortunately, are not the kind one can turn into a book, neatly set out by date. However, they do provide the background for these stories, and help me to at least get the year, the places, and the people, straight.

At the outset, I must record the enormous debt I owe to the people of the Kitikmeot region, the Kitengmiut. From the time of my arrival in their country, they welcomed me to their land, patiently introduced me to their complex language, and shared with me the stories of their land and traditions of their culture.

Out of my profound respect for the elders of the Kitengmiut, I have used the orthography of the central arctic, the dialect called Inuinaktun and the spellings of the words as preferred by the elders of my generation and the generation before. We made an exception in the title of the book, using the spelling "igloo", which is an eastern arctic spelling, but recognized the world over, instead of the local spelling "iglu". In the text, however, we used the local version: *iglu*.

Additionally, I salute my travelling companions – Peter Kamingoak, Jack Allonak, Walter Bolt Wikhak, Sam Oliktoak, Alfred Okkaituk, and Alec Algiak. These men guided me over thousands of miles of our frozen land, and shared my life and experiences. I could not have performed my work, and could not have survived away from the settlements, without their help. They earned my unqualified trust in every conceivable situation.

Although this is not a story of my life before coming to the Arctic, I have referred to the foundations for the mission that engaged my energies for this past fifty years. Ordination signified my entry into membership in the family of the Diocese of The Arctic. Canon Harold Webster guided my introduction to the region and the people of the Arctic, and to him I owe an immense debt. Before his death in retirement, he generously bequeathed to me a number of his photographs with permission to publish them. Canon Webster was a superb photographer, who did all his own processing and printing in a time when this could not have been easy. His stunning black and white photos grace this book.

The danger of frostbitten fingers on a cold camera was his experience, and it was mine as well. My Retina 11 camera "lived" under my heavy furs, loaded with Kodachrome film, ever ready to record the beauty of our land and people with speedy bare-fingered operation. Mostly, and serendipitously, I shot slide film, and the resulting images have been used all over the world in presentations, and now can be shared via this book.

While, within the life of the Anglican Church of Canada, the northern mandate of the Diocese of the Arctic had been well established by the time I arrived in the North, substantial interest and support was still generated within the United Kingdom. The British Fellowship of the Arctic, traditionally centred in Leicester, deserves special appreciation for having given our family, among a number of other families, encouragement by practical means, and by prayer, throughout the fifty years of our active service. We, and the Diocese, are grateful for this support.

Throughout the lengthy process of preparation of *Igloo Dwellers Were My Church,* the assistance of Page Burt has proved indispensable. Page is a long-time Northerner and close family friend who has served as editor for this book. Author of *Barrenland Beauties,* which is a colour field guide to arctic plants, Page is the staff naturalist for Bathurst Inlet Lodge, and has accompanied her editorial skills with the background of a professional biologist, sharing her knowledge of the more scientific aspects of the arctic fauna and ecological habitats.

The Honourable Jake Ootes, Member of the Legislative Assembly for Yellowknife Central, and Minister of Education for the Government of the Northwest Territories, has written the Foreword for this book, for which I am most grateful.

Additional thanks to my family for their assistance in all aspects of the development of this book, from researching photos to final proofing of the manuscript.

Igloo Dwellers has been professionally designed in the North, by Outcrop Communications Ltd., and the support of several companies and individuals have made this possible. Among these are Bathurst Inlet Lodge, Trish and Glenn Warner, Page Burt and Kanuyak Enterprises, Outcrop Communications Ltd., and Kingaunmiut Ltd.

I would like to thank Dr. Tom Beck, another Northerner who is held in high esteem by Inuvialuit and Inuit alike, for his advocacy on my behalf and assistance in locating a publisher.

Finally, I would like to particularly acknowledge the courage of Dr. Ashis Gupta of Bayeux Arts Publishing in accepting the manuscript of this book (by an unknown first time author) for publication, and for guiding us through the final steps of preparation.

Unless otherwise noted, all photographs in this book
were taken by John R. Sperry.

Chapter 1

Ordination

In May of 1950, the city of Winnipeg was fighting for its life against the most devastating Red River flood in its long history. Sandbags lined the banks of the river and stood against the walls of many buildings. People worked endless hours sandbagging and shoring up dikes to protect the city. The slightest rise or fall of the water level mesmerized and held the sleepless interest of tens of thousands of people. A way of life and the future of many people hung on a precarious balance trembling with the slightest movements of the muddy river lapping against the dikes and dams.

On May 27, I was a passenger on the Canadian National transcontinental train from Eastern Canada. The carriages crept

ABOVE: Reverend John R. Sperry, ordained for Arctic Service.

into the stricken city at a snail's pace. I peered out of the window, astounded at the destruction before my eyes.

The flood was uppermost in everyone's mind. As a result, events at the St. John's Anglican Cathedral a few days later failed to attract much attention. However, for some of us those events would have a lifelong significance. On May 30, Donald Ben Marsh was consecrated as the second Bishop of The Arctic. The following day, two young ordinands, Donald Whitbread and I, knelt before the new Bishop, and were ordained for a ministry in the Church of God in the farthest North. A new page turned in the history of the Diocese of the Arctic.

The ordination sermon dwelt on the hardships and dangers that lay ahead for us. This theme had a rather poignant significance due to the silent presence of two witnesses to the costs of ministry in the North. In the church burial grounds, no more than twenty yards from where we knelt, lay the earthly remains of Canon Jack Turner and Bishop Isaac Stringer.

Canon Turner's outstanding service as a pioneer missionary in the north of Baffin Island was cut short by an accidental bullet wound at Moffet Inlet. Every effort was made to save him, including a heroic para-rescue attempt by the Royal Canadian Air Force. Sadly, his wound was too serious, and he died in Winnipeg after his evacuation.

Bishop Stringer became famous in the popular press, not for his missionary work in the Northwest, but because, during starvation times among his Indian companions, he was reduced to eating his boots (skin moccasins).

Neither of these pioneers was foremost in our minds that day. The ordination service was solemn, beautiful, challenging, and a bit frightening. Whitbread and I left the Cathedral amid the prayers and good wishes of all. Many looked at us wistfully as though we were bound eventually to fall off the edge of the frozen world, never to be seen again. I think we both quietly felt that we had been "separated" by the Holy Spirit in apostolic tradition. We hoped that, by the grace of God and a bit of common sense on our part, we might live to see a few years of useful service for our Lord.

Whitbread was assigned to the Eastern Arctic, and I, to the West. A few hours after the service, we parted, going our separate ways into the North. Whitbread accompanied the Marshes to Toronto, and then headed north to his posting in Arctic Quebec, where he reopened the mission at Port Harrison.

I boarded the train for Edmonton, and from there flew one thousand miles north to Coppermine, on the shores of the Arctic Ocean.

Wide geographical separations between missionaries were the norm in those days. Canon Webster of Coppermine and Canon Turner had jointly spent fifty years in Arctic service, but they never met. In that era, it was a case of "East is east, and West is west, and never the twain shall meet." However, the airplane was soon going to change all that.

At the time, missionaries in the Diocese of the Arctic signed a contract for a period of five years of continuous service in the Arctic, without furlough. Upon completion of this time, we were granted a six-month break.

The stipend for a single man was fourteen hundred dollars a year, out of which one was expected to provide for heat and light, food, clothes, and other necessities. We accepted this as a divine commission, and espoused the philosophy, "The Lord will provide". Any untoward emphasis on monetary remuneration, in light of the "Great Commission", was considered somewhat sordid.

So we went forth, so to speak, anxious to meet and greet the people who remained the focus of so much speculation in our minds. And there was another question that cast its shadow over our sense of anticipation. Those we were about to meet, would they be equally anxious to see us? Would we be welcome assets to these northern communities, or merely two more agents of foreign cultures?

Chapter 2

Nuna - the Land: A Place to Be

The land we lived in is called the Canadian Arctic. "Arctic" is a generalized term that means an area with an underlay of permanently frozen ground which is home to low-growing shrubs, north of those areas where larger coniferous trees like spruce, fir, and pine are able to grow.

It is particularly difficult to describe Canada's Arctic and sub-Arctic briefly, because of the vast differences in regional characteristics. The mouth of the Mackenzie River might, in ecological terms, be classified as sub-Arctic, yet it is far north of the southern coast of Hudson Bay, which is clearly, ecologically, Arctic.

The Arctic Circle lies at 66° 30' North latitude, and is defined as a

ABOVE: The beauty of the land enriches our lives. J.R. Sperry and
Cynthia Chalk on Bird Island, Bathurst Inlet. Photo: Page Burt.

series of points on the earth's surface north of which on the shortest day of the year, December 21, the orb of the sun is entirely below the horizon. Conversely, on June 21, the longest day, the sun is entirely above the horizon for twenty-four hours. Due to the tilt of the earth in its journey around the sun, the land above the Arctic Circle experiences constant daylight in the summer, and constant darkness in winter. The farther north you are, the longer the twenty-four hour daylight or darkness lasts.

During our years at Coppermine, located 5o north of the Arctic Circle, we experienced six weeks of continuous daylight, and in winter, six weeks of darkness. This daylight or darkness is not total. In summer, the sun is above the horizon for long periods of time, and just below it only briefly, producing long sunsets and sunrises, and a short twilight period. In winter, the opposite happens; the sun is just below the horizon, creating twenty hours of darkness and about four hours of a lovely twilight, with delicate bands of colours girdling the sky when the sun is just below the horizon.

The Arctic gives birth to all manner of myths. One reads of "the land of eternal snows", and of "iglu dwellers" with the inference that they live in houses of snow (*igloo* or *iglu*) year round. In the inhabited areas of the Canadian Arctic, all the snow melts in the summer (apart from patches in sheltered valleys). Therefore, snowhouses were habitable only until late May at best. The eastern Arctic spelling "*igloo*" is recognized the world over, and therefore was used for the title of this book, but the people of the central Arctic spell it "*iglu*", and that is the spelling adopted in the text.

Winter certainly predominates here. Snow usually falls in September, the lakes are frozen by October, and, depending upon latitude, tides, currents, and winds, the sea freezes by December. The Eskimo (*Inuinaktun*) word for "winter," *ukiuk*, is also the word for "year."

Northern Canada includes large tracts of Arctic and sub-Arctic terrain. The "Arctic" includes the High Arctic islands, an archipelago that reaches to latitude 83o North, the very top of our continent. The Sub-Arctic includes the upper limits of the vast coniferous forests that form a mantle around the upper edge of the temperate zone, from Alaska to Quebec in North America. At the northern limits of the coniferous forest lies the "treeline", a ragged and indistinct line where scraggly spruce trees give way to low tundra vegetation. This ragged line extends from the northwestern edge of the Mackenzie Delta southeast to the southern coast of Hudson Bay. Winter temperatures in the forested areas can average lower readings than in the treeless barrenlands, but the latter experience fierce winds, producing a "chill factor" sometimes approaching -100o C.

In an era when the threat of global warming is a preoccupation of climatologists and laymen alike, it is interesting that the Arctic, like many other regions, has had its share of extremes of heat and cold throughout the millennia.

In addition, due to continental drift, the location of today's Arctic landmasses was not always in polar regions, but at times located in tropical or temperate zones. Deposits of coal along the coast to the west of Paulatuk, and at Pond Inlet on the north end of Baffin Island in the Eastern Arctic, and the remains of fossilized trees on Axel Heiberg Island in the High Arctic provide evidence of a primeval age when the present barrenlands were forested, and the climate was mild.

Within the last 150,000 years, northern North America has been covered by a series of continental glaciations, vast ice sheets that in places attained a thickness of two to five miles. Strangely enough, the center of ice of the latest, the Laurentide or Wisconsin Glaciation, was located in the Keewatin/Kivalliq region, to the west of Hudson Bay, and advanced on the Arctic coast from the southeast, not the north. The latest of these ice sheets retreated from parts of the central Arctic coast no more than eight to ten thousand years ago, leaving a land totally denuded of vegetation, with the very skeleton of the land sculpted by the passage of rocks and sand gripped in the thick ice. The ice caps of Greenland, the Arctic islands, and Baffin Island are remnants of these great ice sheets.

As one travels by plane over Nunavut and the Northwest Territories, the immense panorama unfolds — soaring mountains and huge glaciers calving icebergs into the sea. Then, there are the parallel ridges of ancient beaches, strandlines caused by the sea as the land rose after being relieved of the weight of the ice. Along the Arctic and Hudson Bay coasts there are vast sedge marshes, nesting ground of millions upon millions of waterfowl and shorebirds. There are rolling hills and immense basalt ridges and plateaus, bisected by roaring rivers with waterfalls cutting deep gorges in the land. It is a land both terrible and beautiful, inspiring awe in all who experience it.

About one third of the mainland of Nunavut and the Northwest Territories is fresh water, in ponds, lakes and rivers. This is a bit surprising when one learns that the precipitation (both rain and snow) averages 11 to 14 inches (71 - 88cm) per year, making the area ecologically a desert. However, in the Arctic, the land is underlain by permafrost, permanently frozen ground, which thaws to a depth of only a few inches or feet in summer. Permafrost traps water on the land; it cannot percolate into the ground, and collects in ponds and lakes, or runs off in streams and rivers. Five huge river systems and countless smaller ones drain the interior barrenlands, carrying huge quantities of fresh water to Hudson Bay and the Arctic Ocean. In a world where the water supply is increasingly a serious problem, Canada is exceedingly fortunate.

For the Church, the ecclesiastical description for this land of wonder was simply, "The Diocese of The Arctic", as established in 1933. The Diocese of The Arctic covers some 1.5 million square miles, and is the largest Anglican diocese in the world. It includes the northern third of the province of Quebec (then known as "Arctic Quebec", but now called Nunavik), and the whole of both Nunavut and the Northwest Territories.

Due to an Act of Parliament (the Nunavut Act), negotiated as part of the settlement of Inuit land claims in Canada, the Northwest Territories split into two territories on April 1, 1999. The Inuit homeland in the Eastern Arctic is called "Nunavut", a beautiful word meaning "our land". The remaining land in the west has for the time being kept the name Northwest Territories, but this may change as more of the land claims in the west are settled.

During 1999, Nunavut became a self-governing body with a Legislative Assembly, elected representatives, and a bureaucracy all its own.

During our time in Coppermine (now known by its traditional name of Kugluktuk), we experienced the seasons firsthand, as does anyone living in an Arctic community. The short summers, only two months in length, could be very hot, up to 38° C (100° F). These warm weather "breaks" were never as welcome as they would seem. During the warm weather, the mosquitoes, perennial pests of the North, emerged by the millions, and attacked man and beast with equal ferocity. Fortunately, Arctic mosquitoes carry no diseases, but certainly can drive the animals to distraction. They are a staple of the diets of many species of small tundra birds, and especially important to young shorebirds. They are also important pollinators of many species of Arctic plants.

Springtime in the Arctic was (and is) always a time for celebration. The snow melts, the sea ice "candles", splitting into linear crystals. These shatter and fall into the water to tinkle musically against the edge of the deteriorating ice floes, creating a delicate Arctic symphony.

Rivers disgorge themselves of ice and flow madly to the sea, and the birds arrive in vast numbers to enliven the air with courtship and song. The land bursts into bloom as Arctic flowers carpet the landscape in all their miniature beauty. It is a time of richness of life on a grand scale. Where else could one wish to be?

Chapter 3

From Whence Came They?

Anyone who has experienced the Arctic, or even has developed an academic interest in the area will have some curiosity about its first inhabitants. The culture is so unique, signs of occupation so permanent, and the conditions for life so hazardous, that it inspires admiration and enquiry. How did these people get here? What is their history? How could they possibly survive in this harsh land?

Research has suggested that the ancestors of today's Inuit came into North America fairly recently, after the great Ice Age, and that they migrated across the Bering Land Bridge from Asia, probably seeking new hunting grounds. We believe they chose to move into the treeless tundra and to follow the Arctic coast for two reasons.

ABOVE: Drum dance among the Inuinait, dressed as first encountered by the Canadian Arctic Expedition, ca. 1917. Photo: Canadian Arctic Expedition.

First, they were accustomed to a marine-based culture with the hunting of sea mammals an important part of their existence. Second, early Indian hunting groups already occupied the forested areas to the south. These Indian (now called Dene, or by their correct ethnic names) groups tended to be more warlike than the new people walking into their land. In addition, they knew the terrain and the game and had well-established hunting areas.

Geologists estimate that some twenty thousand years ago an ice-free corridor existed between two major ice sheets; the Cordilleran in the northwest and the Laurentide (or Wisconsin) Ice Sheet, in eastern North America, extending south past today's Great Lakes. The earliest Paleo-Indian hunters wandered down that ice-free corridor, roughly where the Yukon is situated today. Eventually, they spread throughout both North and South America, with the exception of the Arctic.

Other speculations include the theory that human arrivals from Asia travelled from the Bering Straits down the western coastal areas by sea. Indeed, it is an accepted theory that all aboriginal peoples of both North and South America had their origins in Asia. These people share with their Asian ancestors a purplish mark on the coccyx of newborn infants. This spot gradually disappears as the child grows older.

Archaeologists studying in the Arctic are fortunate in that the frigid climate acts as a preservative and signs of human habitation are only rarely cloaked by thick vegetation.

Beginning in the Bering Straits area of coastal Alaska (Cape Krusenstern) and at Onion Portage on the Kobuk River, developing Arctic cultures have been identified and catalogued, resulting in a fairly comprehensive pattern and rudimentary timetable. It is estimated that the first Paleo-Eskimos were found in present-day Alaska some four thousand years ago. From there, they gradually migrated eastward until they occupied much of the Arctic.

One significant group, discovered by the distinguished ethnologist, Diamond Jenness, was given the name "Dorset" from the locality where it was first recognized near Cape Dorset in southeastern Baffin Island. Ancient campsites from that era, created by the Dorset people, occur over huge areas of the Arctic, and even south of the present treeline. These sites offer a wealth of small, finely crafted artifacts, hunting implements, ornaments, tools, and other articles that have suggested a strong emphasis on shamanistic practices.

The Dorset people were replaced by a new migration from coastal Alaska - a people who had developed a whale hunting lifestyle. This group is known as the "Thule" people, after Ultima Thule in Greenland. During a warming climatic period, the bowhead whale gradually extended its range into the central Arctic, and they were followed by the Thule. The presence of large sea mammals required a cooperative hunting strategy but also assured an ample supply of food. This made it possible for the Thule to live through the winter in the High Arctic, where they experienced several months without sun. The abundance of food from a large whale also made it possible for people to live in villages of up to a hundred people, constructing semi-permanent houses. The Thule dominance of the Canadian Arctic extended from about 1000 until the late 1600s.

Then, beginning in 1650 AD, a cooling period, referred to as the "Little Ice Age", changed conditions for the Thule, and brought an end to winter whale hunting. As a result, the Thule are thought to have modified their hunting techniques to utilize the smaller sea mammals (belugas, narwhals, and seals) as well as land mammals such as the caribou. The High Arctic camps were used less often and finally not at all, and the Thule gradually changed into the people known today as the modern Inuit.

Further study, research, and the development of better archaeological techniques will fill in the gaps of our knowledge of these hardy and resourceful peoples. However, it is clear that varying climatic changes have drastically affected the people of each successive culture. The uncertainty of food supplies, a fact that threatens all hunting peoples, together with the accidents and fatal injuries associated with the hunt, at times must have brought enormous hardship upon the scattered camp dwellers. Life for the Dorset and Thule was precarious indeed.

Each culture had its own style of creating tools and implements, and these objects reveal a startling similarity. An arrow point, a burin, or harpoon head from one site within the culture may be almost identical with similar artifacts, perhaps found two or three thousand miles away.

Notwithstanding, isolated groups, if cut off from their neighbours for any length of time, or deprived of the wisdom and skill of their elders by death or misadventure, may suffer alarmingly.

Thanks to the long-remembered stories and oral histories of the Baffin islanders, as well as historic research in recent years, there is one example of such an epic which illustrates this point.

Some one hundred and fifty years ago a shaman of considerable influence, Qillaq, lived on Baffin Island. He saw, in a vision, strangers living far to the northeast. No one had any knowledge of these people, but Qillaq felt drawn to find them. He managed to persuade a number of families to follow him and a pilgrimage started. The accounts of the long trek, which lasted some five years, with disagreements, violence and desertions, are not always consistent. But it appears not more than a dozen folk finally reached the shores of northwestern Greenland.

The Inuit they encountered there must have seemed a pathetic and impoverished group barely eking out an existence. They lacked the sophisticated hunting implements of Qillaq's group. They had no *kayaks* for open water hunting, no *kakivaks* (leisters or fish spears), nor hooks for fishing, and did not use the bow and arrow. Qillaq's group taught the Polar Eskimos how to use all these implements, and their use quickly spread throughout Greenland. Obviously, the reintroduction of these necessities improved the living standards of the people in that isolated region.

It is an unfortunate fact that, in this age of rapid technological growth, the traditional wisdom and skills of earlier generations can often seem of little use.

We need to be reminded perhaps how matters stood when, on equal terms, the Thule migrants from the west were measured against European migrants from the east. The location was Greenland, where the Norseman called Eric the Red, exiled for manslaughter, came to settle in 985 AD. It was about the same time that the Thule people arrived on Greenland's northwest shores.

The Nordic sagas record violent and peaceful contacts with the local inhabitants. However, the success of these colonies remained dependent upon periodic resupply from their homeland. Unfortunately, the cooling climate and more extensive ice cover on the sea reduced the number of ships supplying the area from Norway, and the colonists fell on hard times. By the fifteenth century, the European Norse had completely disappeared whilst the Arctic migrants, despite their difficulties, survived. Indeed, the Norse were not the last Europeans to pay a mortal price for lack of assimilation into well-proven native survival methods.

Chapter 4

What's in a Name?

"What's in a name?" asked Juliet in William Shakespeare's *Romeo and Juliet,* a play written four hundred years ago. This question is certainly asked today, with regard to Canada's Arctic inhabitants, especially in an age when respect for ethnic sensibilities and political correctness are so important.

When the Norse adventurers in their long ships arrived in Greenland, and later on the coasts of North America, they came across other occupants with whom they shared both peaceful and contrary relations. The Norse referred to them as "Skraellings" for reasons generally unknown. The same word apparently applied to both the Beothuk Indians of Newfoundland as well as to their

ABOVE: Jane Kogliak, fur-fringed beauty. Photo: Canon Harold Webster

northern neighbours.

But the name which gradually gained worldwide acceptance for these northern neighbours was "Eskimo". The word "Eskimo" developed either from the Algonquian-related Abenaki "Eskiquimantsic" or the Chippewa "Ashlimegu". Both refer to "eaters of raw flesh". Undoubtedly, this term, from the Indian standpoint, was not meant to be complimentary although, unknowingly, it served to describe these northern neighbours (and traditional enemies) with a uniquely apt designation.

The human body can sustain itself in reasonable health whenever its diet includes the vitally necessary Vitamin C. The Arctic barrenlands are the one region in the inhabited world bereft of agricultural possibilities, owing to its foundation of rock or permanently frozen sub-soil.

The more southerly areas of the tundra support several species of low scrub berries. Due to the short season and the fact that they are soon buried in the snow, these provide a very limited "dessert" indeed. But the staple food of the Arctic peoples is from the harvest of the land and waters and into that food chain Vitamin C enters unhindered.

When the flesh of these creatures, seals, fish, caribou and others is eaten uncooked, the body can make Vitamin C, and dietary balance and health are assured. However, civilization and European culinary practices demanded cooking one's food, even overcooking it. This destroys Vitamin C, and scurvy may result, ending often in death.

Later, with the arrival of southern traders, trappers and others, particularly in the western Arctic and on the west coast of Hudson Bay, the term "husky" was used to refer to the Eskimo people. This term had no relationship to the husky dog, but was in common usage in the 30s and 40s in a complimentary fashion, recognizing the sturdy frame and physical strength of these hardy people.

I once asked an older hunter why, when he was young, the people of his generation were called "huskies" by the whites. He responded by sticking out his chest, flexing his muscles and saying, "Because we are tough and strong". It has been many years since I heard this term used, but, at that time, it was rarely more than a colloquial reference of obvious admiration.

These days there is a perception that the word "Eskimo" is derogatory and must be replaced by the word "Inuit". Inuit is a term from the language of the people of the Arctic. In their language, a succession of meanings is expressed with separate components that compress whole sentences into one word, the root or stem identifying the basic meaning. For the concept of "life", for example, the stem inu- signals every possible later combination that has to do with living. *Inuyuk*, for instance, means, "he/she lives". A living human being is an *inuk*; and the plural for people is *inuit*.

In any language there are usages that identify other beings, especially if they are human and one is not sure of their ethnic category but is aware of their location. There is a suffix that serves the purpose for a known place of existence whoever the inhabitants are. The suffix -*miut* simply means "people of". The inhabitants of Ottawa, for instance, become the *Ottawa-miut*.

"Inuit" was originally a generic term used to describe human beings of any ethnic category. Thus, in the Bible translated in various Eskimo dialects, the word "inuit" is applied to all humankind, without exception or qualification. When Jesus fed 5000 "inuit" - the word for "people" as translated in the New Testament - they certainly were not fur-clad hunters who had had a poor day at the seal holes!

In the Arctic itself, particularly in the central and western areas, the people seem to prefer referring to themselves in specific terms according to their regional identities. But, in hearing the English language they still accept the word "Eskimo" without embarrassment.

Some years ago, the Committee for Original People's Entitlement, based in the Mackenzie Delta, produced a grammar and dictionary for three major dialects for people of the Western Arctic. This linguistic initiative researched local preferences and stated the following in the prefaces in each of their six publications: "In this series of publications the word 'Eskimo' is used rather than 'Inuit' to describe the indigenous people of the Arctic because it is the word that Western Arctic people largely prefer."

Indeed, there are different and specific regional appellations that are insisted upon with some pride. The Arctic Alaskans refer to themselves as *Inupiat*. The Mackenzie Delta folk call themselves *Inuvialuit*, and the central Arctic Coast dwellers term themselves, *Inuinait*. In the more heavily populated Eastern Arctic (Nunavut) the early word, *Inumagiktut* ("truly people") does not seem to have wide usage; Inuit is now used.

In my own experience of half a century in the North, much of which was lived before political sensitivity about ethnic titles became such an issue, being called an "Eskimo" was a salutation of considerable pride. Even today there are indications that the term may regain some of its earlier usage. Possibly the people themselves may realize that had their ancestors not been Eskimo (eaters of raw meat), then there would be no "inuit" (living human beings) surviving to tell the tale today!

All this may not be too important an issue today, but historically may allow for mutual tolerance when different regions wish to express their own preferences for their own people.

Chapter 5

Fort Hearne, Coppermine, Kugluktuk

My new Arctic home had three names - Fort Hearne, Coppermine, and Kugluktuk. Each of these names has special significance and a place in the history of life along the Arctic coast.

The early name, "Fort Hearne" was used to identify the first trading post at the mouth of the Coppermine River. It commemorated the efforts of Samuel Hearne, one of the earliest white men to travel into the central part of the Canadian Arctic region.

A group of Indians who lived and hunted far to the west of Hudson Bay regularly made the long journey to trade at Fort Prince of Wales (later Churchill). The traders of the Hudson's Bay Company listened avidly to the reports of these Indians. They claimed that, far

ABOVE: Early days, Coppermine (Kugluktuk) in the 1940s.
Photo: Dept. of National Defence.

to the northwest, a great river ran to the coast and along its shores were significant deposits of copper. They had the proof; these trading Indians carried with them samples of high-grade metallic copper, often beaten into knives and other tools.

These reports were chronicled as early as 1715; but not until 1770 was an expedition attempted under the leadership of one Samuel Hearne.

As a youth, Hearne served as a seaman in the Royal Navy. His experiences during the Seven Years War certainly prepared him for the hardships he would later face in the Canadian North. After his naval service, he served as a seaman on Hudson's Bay Company supply ships in Hudson Bay waters before being appointed to the staff at Fort Prince of Wales.

Hearne was chosen by the Company for an expedition to seek out the copper mines far to the northwest. The real objective of this expedition was trade - to establish direct contact with the people living in the interior barrens and along the central Arctic coast.

Hearne made two abortive attempts to reach the country of the fabled copper mines, but each failed due to inexperience or lack of motivation of the guides available to him. Finally, Hearne managed to obtain a competent guide. Matonabee was a Chipewyan leader who knew the country between Great Slave Lake and the coast. He had the respect and obedience of his people, and was interested in guiding Hearne to the mines. As time would prove, he had other motives as well. However, the success of the expedition, without a doubt, depended on the skills of Matonabee.

Hearne essentially travelled as a guest of the Chipewyans; he made no decisions about travel or hunting, and had no control over the actions of his guides. In his journal, Hearne describes the trials and hardships of the journey across the interior Barrenlands to the river later known as the "Coppermine". The surrounding country was rough and there were innumerable lakes. Under those conditions, travel, winter or summer, was difficult indeed.

Hearne's formal "orders" from the Hudson's Bay Company were to travel "in quest of a North West Passage, Copper Mines, or any other thing that may be serviceable to the British Nation in general, or the Hudson's Bay Company in particular; in the year 1770". Evidence of copper was genuine but they never found enough to support creation of a "mine". Discovering the Northwest Passage was a fond hope, which had to await the passing of another century.

Hearne's trip along the Coppermine River was not a pleasant experience. To his surprise, his Indian companions began preparing for war as they travelled, and it became apparent that they had another agenda, so far hidden from Hearne. On July l7th, l77l, they encountered a group of "Eskimo" engaged in fishing at a large set of rapids on the lower Coppermine, about ten miles inland from the mouth of the river.

To Hearne's horror, they attacked and annihilated the entire camp as they slept, killing old and young, men, women, and children. According to his journal, Hearne found himself in a situation of some danger and conflict - if he objected to the attack, he might be regarded as an enemy and killed. If he left the group, either side might kill him. He stayed, an unwilling spectator, appalled at what was happening around him.

After the slaughter, Hearne's group spotted several dogs tied at the tents. They deemed these to be of good quality, and did not harm them, but later regretted not taking a few for themselves. The group, including the shaken Hearne, proceeded downriver to the sea. They saw another camp from a distance, but all but one of the inhabitants fled before they could be caught.

Hearne was not impressed with the lower river, as it was certainly not navigable for anything larger than a canoe. However, he became the first white man to see the Arctic Ocean. This ocean, of course, was long familiar to the native people.

The rapids later became known as "Bloody Falls", to mark the massacre. I learned to refer to them as "the Falls of Blood" to avoid the indignation of any sensitive church people to whom I might describe these events.

Hearne finally returned to Prince of Wales Fort in June of 1782. He had endured much hardship and stark terror on his journeys, and deserves considerable recognition for his success in negotiating touchy situations with his guides.

However, later explorers made scathing comments about Hearne's navigational skills. Dr. John Rae stated that Hearne placed the mouth of the Coppermine about 200 miles north and 100 miles west of its actual location. For all of that, travelling overland from southern Hudson Bay to the Coronation Gulf was a remarkable achievement.

What about the three names for the community itself? The Hudson's Bay Company relocated a post from Bernard Harbour to the mouth of the river in 1928, and the Anglican Mission did the same. Once the actual settlement was established at the mouth of the Coppermine, it was given the name "Fort Hearne" in honour of the explorer himself.

This name did not last long, due to its proximity to a point of land named "Cape Hearne" by John Franklin in 1821. To prevent confusion for navigators in the future, the settlement became known as "Coppermine". This fostered further confusion, as people hearing it assumed that there were actually commercial copper mines in the area, something totally untrue!

In the early 1990s, the community of Coppermine requested a name change reflecting the original Inuit name for the area. They selected the name used for the place where their ancestors gathered for fishing in the spring char runs. The simple word *Kugluktuk*, which means "rapids" or "falls", won the day, and further changes are most unlikely.

As this narrative covers the period during which the community was called "Coppermine", I have used the name Coppermine for all references to the community during the time we lived there.

Chapter 6

Aerial Adventures

On June 20, 1950, I experienced my first airplane ride, from Edmonton, the capital city of the province of Alberta, to Yellowknife in the Northwest Territories. This flight was uneventful but enjoyable. I was quickly to learn more about northern aviation. It was from here that I was to set off for Coppermine. My journey to the north was certainly much shorter and more comfortable than that of Samuel Hearne's, but there were moments when I doubted I would arrive in one piece.

In the days before all-weather airstrips were built to accommodate wheeled aircraft, there had to be either open water or solid ice at both Coppermine and Yellowknife so that ski-equipped or float-

ABOVE: Pilot Ernie Boffa and his Norseman, Coppermine, 1948. Photo: NWT Archives

fitted aircraft could serve both communities. The two communities were four hundred miles apart, and there is a marked difference in temperature over that distance. Because of this, long delays occurred during spring "break-up" and fall "freeze-up" until aircraft could safely operate at both points.

On June 21st, I presented myself at the Yellowknife float base with modest travel baggage and stared at the small single-engine Norseman aircraft. It was in the process of being loaded but I could not see any seats inside the fuselage. Turned out I was correct; there weren't any. The pilot had one, of course, and there was another in front for a passenger. Thinking I might reach Coppermine that same day, I had attempted to be properly dressed, and was wearing a new trench coat (it being summer), and, of course, my clerical dog collar.

I met the pilot. He was small, not too inspiring at first glance, and casually dressed. No uniform. Unknown to me at the time, Ernie Boffa was a proven bush pilot, indeed one of the best the North has ever known. I should have had no worries. Unfortunately, I didn't get the seat beside Ernie, but was given an onion box instead. I looked around me, and - no seat belt! Behind me, all manner of goods and mailbags crammed the plane. The people of Coppermine had been waiting for this treasure trove for weeks. At the very back another unseen passenger, accompanied by a dog, occupied another box. Nothing seemed to be happening. We waited.

Finally, after about half an hour, a youngish man was carried on board and dumped unceremoniously next to me. From his disheveled appearance and slurred speech, it was obvious he had been part of some days of celebration prior to his departure for a mining camp further north. He propped himself next to my until-then-spotless trench coat.

With an earth-shattering roar, the engine started, and we were off. I had my first aerial view of the vastness of Canada's North, which still fascinates me to this day. But my amazement was not to last very long, as my companion required a smoke. There were no restrictions in those days. But his fingers could not grasp the lighted cigarette and it fell to the floor. Foolishly, I picked it up and returned it to his fingers, but he dropped it again. I watched in terror as it rolled, and disappeared down a little hole in the deck to where, I assumed, the fuel tanks were located!

Now fully alarmed, I shouted out the problem to Ernie, who, with a louder yell, somehow alerted the back-seat passenger, who managed to shove a fire extinguisher forward over the boxes. Meanwhile, Ernie fishtailed the aircraft in an alarming manner, in order presumably to see whether or not we were trailing smoke from the slipstream. I grabbed the fire extinguisher, directed it at the hole in the floor, and squeezed the handle desperately.

Thankfully, the belly tanks did not ignite and we flew on. My attempt to squirt the extinguishing liquid through that hole just may have done the trick.

Weeping apologies, my companion draped himself across my shoulder and was violently ill all over my nice new trench coat. I surveyed the damage, and felt too fed-up to care. I did contemplate the fact that my poor trench coat would probably not see another drycleaner for at least five years.

We landed soon afterwards at a mining exploration camp and off-loaded the now-repentant and far more sober passenger. Lighter, we took off and continued north, making one more stop at a lake close to the Arctic Circle. It was an abandoned mining camp with a veteran trapper, George Magrum, serving as caretaker. Ernie had heard by radio that the ice still clogged the Coppermine River, and we would not be able to land. I could return to Yellowknife with him or stay with George until the ice went out. I elected to remain with George.

I stayed with George for six days, and had my first taste of the immense silence of the Barrenlands. I found it a great privilege to stay with this knowledgeable man who mostly lived alone with his dogs and his traps. He was not taciturn - I was regaled with many stories of the North and deeply appreciated the initiation this inter-lude afforded me.

George had shot a black bear, and we lived on black bear stew for every meal. The occasional lake trout broke the monotony.

Finally, Ernie returned, and we took up the journey again, flying north into the glare of the midnight sun. At one in the morning, I finally arrived in Coppermine, which was to be my home for the next nineteen years.

Many more years of Arctic flying in small planes followed; but none matched that first trip in terms of unmitigated terror, and awe at the land over which we were flying. At that time, I wondered whether or not that kind of experience was common in the North. Luckily, it was not.

Chapter 7

Home in a New World

The last leg of our aerial journey to Coppermine passed uneventfully. I did get that last seat for the final part of the journey, and luxuriated on the hard seat, appreciating the existence of a seatbelt!

As the Norseman touched down on the bay and taxied in to shore, everyone in the tiny settlement of Coppermine gathered by the plane with obvious excitement. As I disembarked, I was greeted by Canon Harold Webster and everyone else, strangers though they all were.

Actually, it was all those blue bags of mail, together with boxes and parcels of all description that seemed the most welcome. Everybody had awaited that plane for some six weeks.

ABOVE: St. Andrew's Mission in the 1950s.
Original building combining mission house and chapel.

In 1950, Coppermine was tiny, just an embryo of a settlement. At that time, there were two churches, Anglican and Roman Catholic; there was the familiar red and white Hudson's Bay Trading Post, a government radio and weather station, and a small detachment of the Royal Canadian Mounted Police (non-equestrian, of course, but they did have dog teams.)

Of the native population, only seven families actually lived in the settlement. The majority still lived in hunting camps widely scattered throughout the entire area. These people would not appear until the arrival of winter when the lakes, rivers and sea were frozen and snow-covered, providing safe travelling conditions.

Even when I arrived in late June, the Arctic Ocean was still frozen beyond the river's mouth as the short summer's thaw had barely begun.

Half a century later, Coppermine has grown into Kugluktuk, a thriving community with a population of some fifteen hundred souls. It is replete with administrative departments for every aspect of municipal life, rows of modern houses, roads, vehicles, schools, hotels, an all-weather airport with daily flights, and even a Chamber of Commerce.

However, in June of 1950, I was welcomed to the mission house by Edith Webster, the canon's wife, and their two daughters, Ann and Marguerite. In addition to the house, the mission buildings included two small warehouses and a fish-drying house, all located close to the shoreline.

Then there were the sled dogs, sixteen of them, chained up and snapping at mosquitoes. I soon found out that keeping them fit involved an enormous amount of work; especially fishing. Setting and checking the nets became a daily routine, by boat in open water in summer, and later under the ice when the river had frozen.

Seal hunting was another source of procuring food for the dogs. Seals, however, were not as common around Coppermine as they were further north, and so we depended mainly on fish. There were two main species: the Arctic char (a salmon-trout) and a scaled white fish. The char were more numerous. In later years, these became a gourmet specialty for southern palates, and an admired game fish, which drew sport fishermen to the area.

During the summer, we dried most of the fish by splitting them, removing entrails and spine, and hanging them in the sun and wind to dry. This dry fish (*pipfi*) was stored for use in winter. During the summer, when they were not working, the dogs were only fed the entrails, which seemed to be as acceptable as other, larger morsels!

On my first Sunday, our congregation, both white and Eskimo, gathered in a section of the mission house, which doubled as a visiting area and a chapel. This section held about twenty-five folk and, at that time, was quite adequate.

Everything was in Inuinaktun and totally unintelligible to me, so I took no part in the proceedings, but listened intently and observed my new neighbors. Obviously, language study was to be an immediate challenge for me. They used a service book, translated into a far western dialect, which had only a few translations of Scripture passages. But the congregation's response was enthusiastic and, at various breaks in the liturgy, three or four hymns were sung in succession.

In those first few days I soon discovered that, although the short summer was welcome, there was little time for relaxation, and little inclination to go to bed. The midnight sun invites all kinds of evening activity. Somehow, the bracing effect of the "night" air keeps people wide-awake. Thus, people tended to stay up until three or four in the morning and to sleep in until early the following afternoon.

The big event for the entire community was, of course, the arrival of the annual ship bringing the main supplies for the following year.

Each establishment had to place their orders long in advance. The Diocese required that we send out a list of food and other items the previous January, for the entire consignment had to pass through a long journey from the south to its destination. The orders were first delivered to Waterways, Alberta, where they were loaded on a small river barge. This made its way across Lake Athabasca and down the Slave River. The cargo was portaged around the Rapids of the Drowned from Fort Fitzgerald to Fort Smith, and was loaded on another barge for the trip across Great Slave Lake and down the vast Mackenzie River, north to Tuktoyaktuk on the Arctic coast. Here, everything was transferred to a sea-going ship. Finally, when ice conditions allowed, the supply ship delivered all the freight to the central Arctic settlements, including Coppermine. Usually the ship did not arrive until late July or August.

Prior to the arrival of the ship, bringing the heavy building materials, all kinds of other jobs occupied us, including the painting of buildings. We took great care in this, for paint was expensive. If the colours were light, we had to avoid painting when the mosquitoes were thick; otherwise the result was a speckled effect. However, a sharp north wind off the sea ice usually dealt with that problem, discouraging the mosquitoes.

In that summer of 1950, we experienced a brief snowstorm on July 3rd, just enough to remind me where I was. That snow soon melted but, at sea, the season was a bad one for ice and the supply ship, the Fort Hearne, did not arrive off Coppermine until August l4th.

"Shiptime" was fascinating. The ship would usually arrive in the wee hours of the morning, to be discovered by any early risers, who carried the good news around the settlement. Then, we all jumped into frenetic activity, helping unload, checking supplies as they were brought ashore, stacking, sorting, and distributing the cargo. We packed our foodstuffs into the warehouse, and carried our perishables into the house. Few vegetables or fruits (taken for granted in the South) could survive that long journey to the North. We received oranges, double-processed eggs, and potatoes. Otherwise, we did without or enjoyed a modest supply of canned fruits and vegetables. These were heavy, which made them costly to ship.

Then there was the lumber. The bishop had accepted the fact that I might need a room of my own added to the mission house, so lumber supplies arrived for that structure too. Also, he sent building supplies for a modest church building, which was to be separate from the mission house itself.

The building of a Church had become necessary with the growth of our congregation. Previously, when the distant camp people arrived for the Easter festival, the only building in which services could be held for everyone was both improvised and primitive. It was a circular wall of snow blocks, which was too large by far to allow for the normal domed roof of a snowhouse. Long poles placed across the walls allowed for tarpaulins to fashion a temporary roof.

The congregation filled our snowblock "church", but the weather at Eastertime could be very fierce. This shelter was certainly inadequate, and services were uncomfortable, to say the least!

So, carpentry was added to our other fall activities, and we began building the new church. Though construction went swiftly, the fall was short, and it was not roofed in until winter had arrived and mosquito problems were but a dim memory.

Chapter 8

The Summons

In recent years, it has been common for Christians, and indeed for others, in describing their personal life experiences, to refer to them as their "journey". But then, for a missionary, when that journey appears to end up in a location a bit out of the ordinary, the question invariably is: "Did the Church send you up there?" The simple answer is a decided "No!" There was never a sort of ecclesiastical tribunal that sentenced missionary aspirants to a number of years for labour in some frontier Gulag.

The Church considered and accepted for frontier service those who appeared to receive a Call, and gave evidence that it was genuine and had potential. For a good number of years the arctic

ABOVE: Sperry brothers, Roy and Jack with Rob.

regions seemed to attract the attention and interest of volunteers mainly from Europe. Nearly all the Anglican missionaries came from the British Isles; the Roman Catholic Oblate missionaries came from Continental Europe; and the servants of the Hudson's Bay Company, from Scotland and the Isles, or from Newfoundland.

I was born in 1924 into a sound, hardworking home heavily influenced by the Methodist and Anglican traditions. My family hailed from Leicester, England, and my father was in the shoe-making business.

The first home I can remember was close to a Methodist Church (where my brother and I became Wolf Cubs) and an Evangelical Free Church, Melbourne Hall, where we attended Sunday School. Attendance at the Methodist or Anglican Church of our grandparents depended upon which of their homes our parents were visiting at the time on a Sunday.

Shortly before World War II broke out, Melbourne Hall invited an Australian evangelist, Lionel Fletcher, to conduct a series of meetings. On a Sunday afternoon, our Sunday School was assembled to listen to this enthusiastic preacher.

We had heard the story of the Gospel many times before. However, that afternoon it was presented in a far more dynamic manner, demanding of a personal response. At the invitation to surrender our young lives to Christ, as I recall, no one seemed to hesitate, probably more from the emotion of the moment than with any "counting of the cost". But, by the grace of God, that happening had a very special meaning for me. In the reality of a personal act of faith, I took a major and deliberate step toward my "journey" and my commitment to God.

Missionary work had a vital place in Church life some seventy years ago. My Methodist grandmother always kept a missionary box on the sideboard. My Anglican grandmother's Church of St. Barnabas supported missions in remote places like Tristan da Cunha. Missionary societies were numerous and, due to various visits from mission "fields" (as they were called at the time), my interest grew. Why the Eskimo should ever become my special concern, I shall never know; but they did.

At the tender age of fifteen, I started a search to discover what current Society might be at work in so distant a field of mission as the Canadian Arctic. Eventually, I was given the address of a gentleman by the name of Webster, who presided over a modest Anglican mission hall near Blackpool. His son Harold was a missionary in the Diocese of the Arctic, stationed in Coppermine in Canada's Northwest Territories.

I wrote to the Reverend Harold Webster in far-off Coppermine, telling him of my sense of interest in mission work in the Arctic. And, in his kindly reply (without suggesting that I should start packing!), he promised to keep me in his prayers.

I am often asked what phases in my personal experience best prepared me for Arctic service, and my answer, always is, "Every one!" In my youth, I always participated in a lively Church fellowship. This included early days of Christian development, where "sharing the Good News" was expected and encouraged. Regular patterns of prayer and Bible study, and a circle of like-minded friends and acquaintances combined to shape for me a positive foundation for what lay ahead.

Then, World War II came, and with it major changes in the lives of all Britain's people.

My generation was collectively "called" to serve in the military, a very necessary, but secular, mission. Upon joining the Royal Navy at the age of eighteen years, I received basic training as a seaman. Following this training, I was posted to a destroyer escort ship, *HMS Verdun*. For the following two years, we were constantly on convoy duties in northern waters. It was here that I developed a tremendous respect for the sea.

Exposure to life in the cramped and often miserable conditions of a ship in wartime proved to be an appropriate preparation for what lay ahead. It was an excellent (though not always pleasant) training ground for the future.

Edmund Peck, a veteran pioneer missionary in the North, had previously served in the Royal Navy during a considerably harsher time, in the 1850s. In his writings, he often affirmed his appreciation for what his time in the Navy did for his later ministry - both for testing his Christian commitment, and for practical challenges.

Following the end of the war in Europe, I was posted to a minesweeper flotilla on the *HMS Hare*, bound for the China Sea and Japan. Our visits to many ports en route and seeing sights of destruction and devastation (including the atom-bombed cities of Nagasaki and Hiroshima) increasingly encouraged my desire to share the message of the Prince of Peace to a broken world.

When the War ended, my early sense of missionary interest in the Arctic had faded. I enrolled at Emmanuel College, a missionary training college in Birkenhead. This interdenominational school prepared students for service under various denominations. At that time, ordination occupied no place in my thoughts.

However, one of the visiting lecturers at Emmanuel College was the Rev. F. J. Taylor, (later the Bishop of Sheffield). His words affected me deeply, reinforcing that long-forgotten teenage sense of enthusiasm for distant missions. I listened to him with growing commitment.

Reverend John Drysdale was Principal of Emmanuel. He was a Scot who, possessed by a keen sense of the challenge of missionary enterprises, added to our academic work spartan-like routines calculated to test the fibre and commitment of all who came under his authority. He knew the mission field would require strength within, and was determined to build it.

During that first Easter term, eight of us were selected to engage in a trek across northwestern England, on foot, rain or shine. We hauled a wheeled cart with painted texts on its sides, advertising our purpose. Similar to early initiatives of the Church Army, this was an evangelistic venture with pre-arranged stopovers for specific mission weekends. One stopover was a little Anglican mission hall near Blackpool.

I had long forgotten all about that enquiring letter I had sent to Coppermine some ten years earlier.

Hauling our cart, we pulled up at the mission, where we were greeted by the senior Mr. Webster. He said, "I have just recently heard your group was coming. I noticed that one of your group bears the name 'Sperry'. Is there a 'Sperry' among you?"

I sheepishly held up my hand and stepped forward. He took me aside and informed me of an amazing turn of events. "Last summer," he said, "the ice was so unbroken on the Arctic Ocean that the supply ship could not get into Coppermine. The winter supply of coal could not be delivered for the mission there."

"Without coal, my son and his family faced a difficult winter, and would have been a burden on the local people. The Bishop directed him and his family to fly south, taking early furlough. They are here, visiting us, and you shall have an opportunity to speak with my son!"

There they were in the house, and found time to share stories about their life and mission, illustrating it with their personal photographs. Canon Webster was an excellent photographer, and these were a beautiful record of life in the Arctic.

Archbishop Temple, I think, once said, "I cannot always understand how prayer really works, but when I pray all sorts of coincidences seem to happen to my friends." This, for me, was an exceptionally profound (and appreciated) "coincidence".

That visit affected me deeply, and became yet another step on the journey, reinforcing my feelings regarding my "Call" to Arctic service.

Reverend Taylor, whose words had so affected my vision of the future, later interviewed me on behalf of the Bishop of the Arctic, Archibald Fleming. The door to Canada and the Arctic was opening. I gradually came to believe that I could best serve if ordained to the sacred ministry.

My parents both took no special steps to influence my brother and me in our choice of vocations after the war. My father offered me a position in his firm, but, upon my decision to follow a very different calling, offered and always maintained his unqualified support.

I think my parents always realized that, should my vocation take me to the Arctic, it would mean years of separation, and the lack of an opportunity to watch their grandchildren grow up. My brother Roy Sperry, who was also committed to the support of Christian missions, moved to Nigeria for many years, where he worked as an accountant. Though many families hoped that peace would bring an end to the separations so common in wartime, it seemed our family would have to endure more separations. Our parents understood, and accepted these separations with a spirit and attitude that was exemplary.

I travelled to Canada, to continue my studies at King's College in Halifax, Nova Scotia. After my ordination, I was sent to St. Andrew's Mission, Coppermine, to join Canon Webster, the very person I had written to so many years ago.

Shortly after my arrival, Canon Webster and I shared our "journeys". When I related my encounter under the ministry of Lionel Fletcher, Harold Webster looked at me in amazement. He said, "When I was a young man, I also heard Lionel Fletcher speak! It was his words that challenged me to make the same commitment you have made!"

We looked at each other, and into our minds floated the same phrase: "God moves in mysterious ways, His wonders to perform!"

Chapter 9

The *Kitengmiut* and their Journey

The aboriginal people of the Kitikmeot region are referred to in various ways. Anthropologists call this group the "Copper Eskimo" or "Copper Inuit". In their own language, as members of the human race, they are "Inuit" - living people. More precisely, they are Inuinait, a name by which they identify themselves as distinct from their neighbours both to the west and east. Then, for geo-political purposes, more recently and as a group, they are classified as *Kitengmiut*, meaning "inhabitants of the middle", the central region of the Canadian Arctic.

An enormous challenge awaited (and currently awaits) newcomers to the Arctic with any interest in learning about and relating

ABOVE: Harpoon-equipped seal hunter. Photo: Canon Harold Webster.

to the culture. This beautiful but alien environment is occupied by a people who have, through the centuries, learned how to adapt and survive under extremely harsh conditions. Although their environment may appear simple, their culture is not simple at all.

Although I did not realize it at the time, I was unusually privileged to be able to live and work with the Kitengmiut at this time in the history of the North. I was associating with a group of Inuit who were among the very last people in North America to be introduced to and influenced by our Euro-American/Canadian culture and technology.

In the Arctic, the first meeting of Europeans and aboriginal North Americans took place a millennium ago when the Norse adventurers first came across the Paleo-Eskimo in Greenland. Much later, the natives of Baffin Island experienced unhappy conflicts with Martin Frobisher's three expeditions in the late 16th.century.

In following decades, ships of explorers and whalers sailed into the Eastern Arctic and Hudson Bay, coming into contact with the people that inhabited these coasts and islands. Also, in the west, Russian adventurers and fur traders were penetrating Alaska from Siberia. Gregori Shelekhovik founded the first permanent settlement in 1784, during the reign of Catherine the Second. Almost a hundred years later, in 1867, Russia sold the entire land mass of Alaska to the United States for $7,200,000. Consequently, the sea-hunting coastal natives in both areas had contacts with these foreigners centuries earlier than the "People of the Middle".

In the Central Arctic, Inuit followed a pattern of nomadic life, which included summer hunting inland far from the coast. This isolated them, to a large extent, from outsiders, as most European or Euro-Canadian exploration occurred from ships, in the summer.

Indeed, in that period of history there were a few contacts but none of lasting positive effect. In July of 1771, Samuel Hearne's ill-fated experience with an Inuit group at Bloody Falls on the Coppermine ended in a massacre. John Franklin's arrival at the same rapids, exactly fifty years later, did result in one happier contact. An old man named Terriganiak was fishing at the falls, and was too feeble to run away. As a result, Franklin's Inuit interpreters (hired from the Hudson Bay area) were able to talk to him.

From Terriganiak, the members of the expedition were able to learn more about his people, who they were anxious to contact. But he was the last Inuk they met. Throughout the rest of their expedition, they charted the coastline for 340 kilometers, even travelling to the southern end of Bathurst Inlet. They saw many campsites, but encountered no people. All were inland, hunting at the crossing places on the interior rivers and lakes.

One unique midwinter contact, however, did occur on western Victoria Island in 1851. McClure's ship, the *Investigator*, was engaged in the search for the lost Franklin expedition. On board was a German Moravian missionary, Johann Miertsching. He was to serve as interpreter, if they met native people. The Investigator became trapped in the ice at Mercy Bay on the north end of Banks Island. During the long winter, man-hauled sledge parties were dispatched for local exploration.

Entering the inlet later known as Prince Albert Sound, McClure's men met a band of Eskimos who were seal hunting. Miertsching, despite his very different dialect, managed to assure the peaceful intentions of these strangers and each group studied the other with avid curiosity.

One woman with a baby on her back approached the captain and asked what animal there was that had such a scarlet skin; this pointing to the woolen scarf the captain had around his neck.

Captain McClure promptly took it off and gave it to the woman as a gift. The poor woman, following the customs of her people, realized that a gift of such magnitude demanded a reciprocal gift. But, without anything of value, she tearfully offered him all she had - her baby. The tough-minded captain wept in sympathy as he declined the gift.

So, the general isolation of the Kitengmiut continued, and not until the arrival of the Canadian Arctic Expedition (1913-1918) was a more permanent "foothold" of European culture established in the Central Arctic.

I was fortunate in being appointed to this particular region of the Arctic at this time. I had the rare opportunity to relate to a people whose elders had grown to adulthood without any visible contact with the "benefits" of southern technology. There were older men and women who had from childhood followed the age-old nomadic patterns of their ancestors, seal hunting on the sea ice during the long winter; spear fishing at the stone weirs in the river mouths in spring, and moving inland to hunt land animals in summer.

Their weapons were the bow and arrow, harpoon, fishing leister, and knife. All the utensils in use in the snow houses or skin tents were handmade locally. Lamps and pots were laboriously fashioned from soapstone, and mugs and ladles made from muskox horn. Weapon points were made of bone, slate, antler, or surface copper. Fuel for the stone lamps came from seal blubber or caribou fat. Their clothing was made from animal skins; they had virtually no fabrics at all until the traders came into the area in the 1920s. Even their needles were made of split bone or beaten copper.

The people did do some trading through inland travel routes with other Inuit who came from the east. These people brought a few trade goods from the post at Baker Lake. Also, a small amount of trade goods came in from the west, again brought by other Inuit.

By 1950, of course, much of this was just a memory. Rifles had replaced the bow and arrow and life had become much more manageable. Also, though the people still lived in widely separated hunting camps, their nomadic lifestyle was greatly modified.

As I slowly made progress with the language, I discovered in myself a keen desire to learn more about their lives and the past. The elders were an absolute treasure trove of wisdom and memories. From them I learned of the past - a vivid picture of pre-historic life in the Arctic.

Once they knew I understood them, and their ideas, they had much to say about their culture, practices, and communication with the unseen world. It was evident that their world was one of mystery and magic, with heavy reliance on the shamans. Every serious problem prompted a shamanistic divination or seance to determine a solution.

Knud Rasmussen journeyed across the Arctic from Greenland to Alaska with the Fifth Thule Expedition in 1924. At Baker Lake, west of Hudson Bay, he enquired from one camp elder what his people believed. The simple answer was, "We don't believe anything - we only fear".

As a Christian missionary, I found it important to understand from where the people had come in their former days. I needed an understanding of their world as expressed in their own vocabulary. Such insights were invaluable for the momentous task of translation that lay ahead.

But, even if I did not need to translate, I needed to have respect for the past and for the struggles of people trying to survive in a world of competing powerful spirits. Thanks to the labours of those before me, most people in the area accepted that there was one creator, God. This offered profound deliverance from the earlier fearful uncertainties.

And, there were other studies that made our work easier. Before I was born, Diamond Jenness had carefully chronicled the life of the Copper Inuit as part of his work with the Canadian Arctic Expedition (1913-1918). His years in the Central Arctic, including months spent with a family group in southwest Victoria Island, provided him with an intimate knowledge of the life and culture of the Inuinait.

Ikey Angotisiak Bolt had been another member of the Canadian Arctic Expedition, and certainly helped me to understand the people. An Inupiak from Alaska who later settled in Coppermine, he was a catechist in the Church, and a valued friend to me for many years. Ikey was born at Point Hope, Alaska, among a people long influenced by the whalers and by the southern culture. His accounts of his first meetings with the Copper Inuit when they were virtually untouched by southern "civilization" attested to the magnitude of the changes that swept the North with the arrival of the trade goods. Life went from being very uncertain to being much more secure in a very few years.

It was during the 1950s, before the enormous impact of government investment, together with aggressive exploration for mineral resources, that the language, wisdom, and skills of the elders still had relevance and influence among the people.

Each family, at that time, lived together in one snowhouse or skin tent, with few outside influences or distractions. They communicated in the common language of their ancestors, and the young people learned the culture and its strengths from their parents and grandparents.

Despite the welcome availability of trade goods by that time, there was still room for ingenuity and expertise in fashioning appropriate hunting instruments (harpoons, for example, were not factory-made), and all sleds and dog harnesses were locally produced. People were creative at using trade goods to enhance tools they had made for hundreds of years - buttons could be used to create better fishing lures, and the handles of brass reloaders might be removed and reworked into harpoon heads.

Perhaps most significant was the establishment of a more contented lifestyle. This was the mindset that now rejected the earlier notions that every problem and emergency was caused by the neglect of a taboo or was the work of a malevolent evil spirit. As my travelling companion Alec Algiak related, an approach to any crisis with a clear mind and confidence in seeking a solution is a much-improved option to the fatalism of former times. However, if all fails, it was affirmed, the sovereign Lord may surprise us all with a surprising intervention.

Indeed, in that world, those indomitable descendents of ancient survivors, still living in a most harsh and unforgiving environment, continued to display the best of their traditions and culture. It was due to the privilege of living and travelling with them that I became far more an observant learner than I was a teacher, and profited by this, enormously.

Chapter 10

Their World and Beliefs

The Arctic has been characterized as a land of extremes, a "land of feast or famine". This is very true.

On the Arctic mainland, the great caribou herds, hundreds of thousands strong, transform the Barrenlands into a living, moving landscape during their seasonal migrations. The air is filled with their scent, with the clicking of their hooves and the rumbling of their bellies, the bleats of calves and grunts of the mothers. For a brief time, the land is vibrant with life... and then they are gone, vanished as utterly as though they had never existed at all.

Sometimes the caribou abandon their traditional migration routes without warning or apparent reason. In the time when the

ABOVE: A morning chore - "defrosting" the ice window in an iglu.
Photo: Canon Harold Webster.

ABOVE: The tiny settlement of Coppermine in 1952. At this time, only seven families lived there year-round.

LEFT: St. Andrew's Mission about 1956. Built in 1929, this building served as both mission house and church. Building foundations laid on undisturbed sod above permafrost did not shift whatever the season if tightly sealed with sod around the edges. In winter, a bank of snow blocks added to the insulation.

PREVIOUS PAGE: George Okhena, near Holman, western Victoria Island. The ruff of his hood is wolf, with caribou fur next to his face.

LEFT: Wilberforce Falls on the Hood River, flowing into Arctic Sound, typifies the stunning beauty of the land along the Arctic Coast. *Photo: Allen Kapolak*

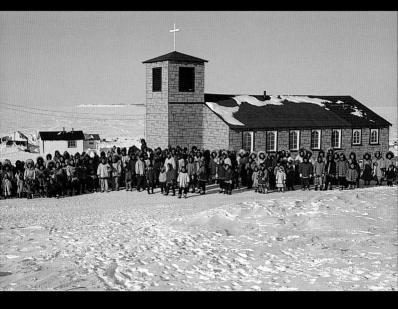

TOP: The new church building, ca. 1950, before tower was added.

ABOVE: Congregation of St. Andrew's Mission in 1960, with "Norman version" of the tower just completed.

TOP: A steeple was added in 1965 …
St. Andrew's Mission with congregation

ABOVE: Sunday worship in St Andrew's
Mission in 1965. Note that the news did

TOP: J. R. Sperry building foundation for a new mission house in 1964. All lumber was shipped from Alberta via the Slave River, Great Slave Lake, the Mackenzie

ABOVE: New mission house in the light of the midnight sun, 1961. The sun remains above the horizon for about a month in June.

Able Seaman Sperry, Royal Navy. 18 years of age. Sperry served on a destroyer escort ship with northern convoys during World War II. After the end of the European phase of the war, he served on a minesweeper in the Pacific.

Elizabeth MacLaren, SRN. Betty Sperry took her SRN (State Registered Nurse) training at the Royal London Homeopathic Hospital and midwifery training, resulting in a SCM (State-Certified Midwife) degree, at several London hospitals, including Queen Charlotte's Hospital.

TOP: Paul Pugatak with frozen seals caught for dog food, at Naloayuk, western Victoria Island.

ABOVE: Annie Kadlun and Jim Koihuk in their spring atigis. Strong faces, yet showing the strain of a hard life on

ABOVE: At Harry Niakoaluk's camp at Nauyat. Left to right: Harry Niakoaluk, Andrew Akoakhiun, Frank Kudlak, Harry Igutak, Flossie Papidluk, Margaret Tangnik, Joseph Alukik, Margaret Ikeguak.

BELOW: Harry Niakoaluk's iglu camp at Nauyat, near Holman. Large porches allowed the operation of stoves for the cooking of an occasional hot meal for the dogs. The toboggan-style sled is a western arctic import.

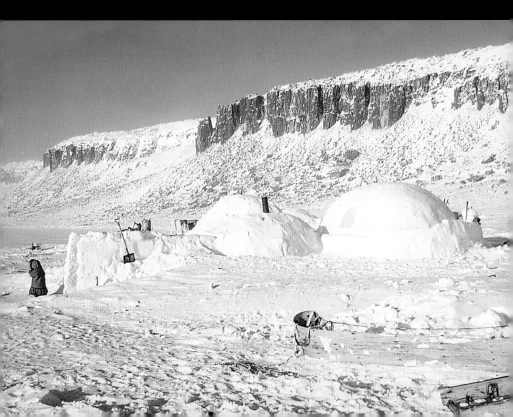

TOP: Mission dogteam, Sperry driving.
The mission dogs were well-cared for.
A healthy, well-fed team could work in the
most severe weather, for days on end.

ABOVE: Skinning caribou in the fall. It
was necessary to hunt, as fresh meat was
never available from the south.

FAR LEFT: Hunting ringed seals for dog food in summer. It was necessary to wait until
mid-August to do this, as prior to mid-August, the seals' blubber is too thin, allowing the

TOP: Teddy Novoligak cutting ice for ice porches or drinking water, on the river ice near Coppermine.

ABOVE: Ice blocks for drinking water, stacked on the ice for dogteam transport to the settlement.

FAR RIGHT: Pulling ice block out of the water. This ice would be stored near the mission house and thawed in a barrel in the kitchen, to be used for drinking and cooking.

TOP: Building an ice porch on the
mission house in Coppermine. Sperry,
Angela Sperry, Jacob Kohotak, and
Frank Ikpakhoak.

ABOVE: Mission house with ice porch.

ABOVE: The ice porch made a marvelous larder, for storage of meat and fresh bread. Bread was taken right out of the oven and quickly frozen in the porch while still hot. It kept beautifully that way.

LEFT: Mission team from the sled, travelling to Minto Inlet on Victoria Island.

Icing sled runners, yet again!

Repairing damaged sled runners with mud or porridge oats.

Adliak loaded with caribou skins, en route to trading post

people of the Arctic hunted by dogteam or by walking inland, the failure of the caribou to appear as predicted could easily result in starvation for those who had travelled to intercept them. Several thousand caribou could pass down one valley, whilst hunters on the other side of a ridge would never know they had passed. People hunted at the traditional caribou crossing places on the rivers. If the caribou used another crossing place, the hunters might miss the only chance at being able to catch them that month, or that year. A failed hunt could mean death.

In the warmth of springtime, scores of plump seals bask in the sunshine beside open leads in the sea ice. However, as the hunters seek those same seals in winter, they are not easily found, as they breathe only at holes in the ice kept open by the repeated passage of their bodies. Snow covers the breathing holes, leaving a white surface completely devoid of any sign of seals. It takes skill and the help of a trained dog to locate these holes. Those who did not find them could suffer extreme hardship.

The Arctic itself - climate, land, and animals - creates a feeling of uncertainty among all people. Its harshness and unpredictability, and the very real dangers of the intense cold, of great predators, and of the unforgiving icy waters that claim lives every year, all combine to inspire utmost respect and even fear. This is true even now, when the world of technology permeates almost every corner of the Arctic.

This uncertainty is reflected and firmly rooted in the language itself. An example is the invariable use of the subjunctive mood of the verb. An example in English would be as follows: One might say, "When we see each other again, we will....." In the Eskimoid language, this would be stated, roughly, "If we see each other again, we will..." The fairly certain "when", used in societies with expected security, becomes the uncertain "if" as the very fabric of life is a matter of doubt.

A glance at a map of the Arctic reveals a wealth of geographic names honouring royalty and the patrons of expeditions, but also reveals names reflecting hardships: Starvation Cove, Desolation Island, Cape Storm, Bad Weather Cape, Bay of God's Mercy, and others. The more ancient names of the people reflect these same hardships....*Inuengnigit* (Dead Man's Island), *Salluit* (Place of Hollow Cheeks, due to starvation), *Inuktugvik*, (Place of Eating Human Flesh).

In this uncertain world, there is an innate sense of the unseen, of external powers that control weather, availability or absence of game animals, and a multitude of dangers that threaten all human existence. These invisible spirit beings, empowered with supernatural influences, were believed to be housed in animals, or sometimes in man, and often were believed to be able to control the environment or the weather.

From the time of the Paleo-Eskimo, people lived with a constant and deep concern for ways to communicate with and placate these powers that ruled over their world. There was no basic understanding of one supreme creator, one God, or even a Great Spirit similar to the belief of the Plains Indians. (The Inuinait did acknowledge Anagafaaluk, a powerful "old lady" who lived in the ocean, but she had no authority on the land.) The spirits, who were present everywhere in that world, sometimes were good, but more often, malignant. They were responsible for everything that happened, the presence or absence of game, good weather and bad, health and sickness, life and death.

The spiritual leadership of these small Inuit groups rested with the shaman, or *angakuk* in Inuinaktun. The shaman was a man or (sometimes) a woman who was recognized as having special powers because he or she could invoke one or more "helping familiar spirits", called naguaguta. Often these were the spirits of animals (polar bears and wolves were favoured), but they could be spirits of humans. The shaman communicated with these "helpers" while in a trance-like state of possession. Often they admitted that they were unaware of what was being said while in the trance. Gestures and words (sometimes in another language) had to be reported once the shaman returned to normal, usually in an exhausted state. If the meaning was still a mystery, the shaman himself interpreted the truth to everyone.

Through the trance experience, the angakuk might claim transmigrational powers such as flying to the moon. The trance created an atmosphere in which the reasons for the trouble would be revealed. The spirits of the dead might express their displeasure, particularly towards anyone who might have broken a taboo. Occasionally, a shaman might expel a malignant spirit, known as a tupilak.

Among the Kitengmiut ("people of the middle"), one group of powerful evil spirits were called *agiuktun* in Inuinaktun. These were invisible to ordinary people, but discernible to the shaman. The angakuk could attack and vanquish these evil spirits, usually in the porch of the iglu. He would go out to do battle with the agiuktun, and return, exhausted, his spears dripping with blood. I have listened to numerous accounts from the elders who, in their youth, witnessed such triumphs.

In those early days, community, family, and personal life was dominated by innumerable taboos (*aglektun*). Each of these, if carefully followed, offered protection from danger. Some, of a general nature, were understood and observed right across the Arctic, while others were more locally enforced. One general taboo was that the meat of land-based animals (the caribou) must never be eaten on the sea ice, and that the sewing of caribou skin clothing must only be done on the land. Likewise, creatures of the sea could not be eaten on the land.

Women could not sew certain garments during the dark days of winter. Children could not play string figures (a form of the cat's cradle games) when it was light. In some areas, the wearing of the slitted wooden or bone snow goggles was forbidden to women, even in springtime, when these goggles provided protection against snow blindness, which is intensely painful.

Some of the shamans were good people who had a genuine concern for their charges, whilst others were charlatans without scruples. The problem was that, in the primitive society of the past, it was all too easy for resentment and revenge to be expressed through the spiritual leaders. Just about anyone in the camp could be singled out and his or her behaviour interpreted as "guilty", should the angakuk bear a grudge.

For example, a rolled-up fur garment (called a kila) was laid on the ground and the spirit of either a living or a dead person, was invited to enter it. The shaman addresses the *kila* with pointed questions, and interprets its answers by whether the bundle becomes heavy or light when lifted, similar to the Ouija Board of our cultures, and with similar dubious authenticity.

In Arctic society, as well as in many other cultures, the spiritual leader of the group, whether called the shaman, medicine man, *angakuk*, or whatever, was the most powerful and feared person in the group, due to his (or her; female shamans were not uncommon) mystical power and contacts with the spirit world. And, of course, as in the case of leaders in the so-called "civilized" societies, competition led to intense jealousy.

Shamans often were intensely jealous of others with the same talents. Curses (*hunianit*) and counter-curses were common. The shaman's most dreadful weapon was the power of the curse; the placing, even at a distance, of a malignant spell on another, resulting in sickness, an accident, bad luck in hunting, deep depression, and even death. Competing curses flew back and forth and the prestige of the shamans involved waxed and waned.

Curses were not peculiar to Inuit, but also were common among the Dene and other Indian groups. In his journal, Samuel Hearne wrote of being asked to put a "whiteman's curse" on an enemy. Matonabbee asked Hearne to put a curse on a piece of paper, which could be sent to the victim, many miles away. Without much conviction, Hearne drew a stick figure of himself (with a top hat) and a sharp arrow or weapon pointing from himself to the enemy. The message was sent, and the recipient glanced at the message, took to his sleeping skins, called his relatives together, and soon died. Such was the immense power of a curse.

This belief in the power of the curse has not disappeared completely in modern times. In the 1960s, I visited an elderly lady from Holman in hospital in the south. A doctor had informed her of her medical condition, speaking through an interpreter who was obviously unacquainted with her dialect. She informed me that the doctor had placed a curse on her, and that she would soon die. She accepted this as inevitable, and was failing by the day. Nothing could convince her that the doctor had done nothing of the sort. En route to Holman and still convinced of her fate, she stayed for a while in Coppermine. After daily visits for counselling and prayer, she suddenly announced that the curse had been lifted and that she would live. She lived at least fifteen years after this event!

The days long ago were undoubtedly times of vivid fear and dread, dominated as the people were in the confusion and complexity of spirit powers, taboos, and the fragility of survival. Even today, despite the complexities and difficulties of existence in our modern society, the elders talk of the all-pervading sense of fear in the past. But none deny their willing acceptance of the Gospel that declared that there was one Creator, a God of love who gifted human beings with a variety of animals for their livelihood and well-being.

In my fifty years in the North, I have yet to hear, from these witnesses or their families, one hint of a desire for an apology for sharing the Good News of that Gospel.

Chapter 11

"Go, and Make Disciples of all Nations."
Matthew 28:19

"Go, and make disciples of all nations." (Matthew 28:19). These words are recorded in the Gospel as a direct command by the Lord Jesus Christ to his followers. To Christians, this divine direction is known as "The Great Commission". It has been responsible for evangelistic movements throughout the history of Christianity. In recent years, however, the Great Commission seems to have fallen into disfavour, as there is a growing feeling that to share the Gospel of Jesus Christ with already-established non-Christian communities is an affront to their human rights and dignity.

However, previous to these shifts in reasoning, missions were an important part of the mandate of Christian churches all over the world.

ABOVE: St. Andrew's Mission service during the Bishop's visit, 1951:
From left: Reverends J.R. Sperry and Robert Douglas, Bishop Donald Marsh, Lay Reader
Ikey Bolt. Note coal stove heater. Photo: Canon Harold Webster.

By the end of the tenth century, Eric the Red had already established the Norse colonization of Greenland. He believed in the ancient Norse gods, but his son, Leif Ericsson, became a Christian. So, in 1000 AD, at the dawn of the first millennium, Norway's Christian monarch, King Olaf, sponsored a mission to Greenland to spread the Gospel.

So reads the saga: "That same spring, King Olaf also sent Leif Ericsson to Greenland to proclaim Christianity there, and Leif went there that summer, and had with him a priest and other teachers..." Christianity was represented in Greenland for some four hundred years, vanishing only with the disappearance of the last known descendants of the Norse colonists.

Nothing was heard from the "lost" colonists of Greenland after the beginning of the fifteenth century.

However, in the early decades of the eighteenth century, Hans Egede had a dream. The Norwegian-born Lutheran minister studied and was ordained in Denmark. At the age of thirty-five, he embarked on a mission that was certainly Christian, yet also held hints of a "search and rescue" intent. Overcoming indifference or outright opposition, Egede finally obtained blessings for his mission from the Bishop of Bergen. On May 12, 1721, accompanied by his wife and family, he set sail for Greenland in the vessel *Good Hope*.

Upon his arrival in Greenland, Egede found no Norse colonist survivors, but did find Greenlandic Eskimos. Once he knew them, he urged that they no longer be referred to as "Skraellings". Reverend Egede found them to be authentic subjects for the sharing of the same Gospel message that had been proclaimed in Greenland so many years before.

He and his family built a mission and settled in. They worked in Greenland for fifteen years - years of study, learning the language, and offering a compassionate ministry. However, after that time, broken in health through much hardship, Hans Egede returned home, accompanied by his family. He died shortly thereafter, but is remembered as the "Apostle to Greenland".

Within a very few years of the establishment of the Lutheran mission in Greenland, another branch of the reformed Church became caught up in the missionary vision for the distant lands of the North.

The Moravian Brethren, spiritual descendents of the earliest reformed Church in Europe, established a missionary tradition almost unequalled in post-Reformation years. Very soon after Hans Egede began his work in Greenland, Moravian brothers arrived to share in the work. However, after making some progress with the Eskimo language, they heard of an "open" field of missionary opportunity in Labrador. The decision was made to establish a mission in Canada.

A brother called Erhardt, accompanied by four other missionaries and a small crew, arrived in Labrador on the vessel Hope, on July 31, 1752. That ship dropped them (seven in all) on shore, and continued on to carry on some trading elsewhere, while the mission party attempted to contact the natives. They were never seen again, apparently killed as unwelcome visitors.

The Moravians continued to work for better contacts and relations in Labrador, and by 1770 had established the first Christian missions among Canada's Inuit. These new initiatives were taken under government sponsorship, which granted 100,000 acres of land to each Moravian settlement, and assured exclusive trading rights to the Brethren. The principal motive for restricting trading was to protect Labrador's native population from the activities of southern whiskey traders. In recent years, the Moravian Missions gladly returned the Settlement lands, once placed under their control, to their rightful owners, the Innu and Inuit of Labrador.

Outside of Labrador, it was almost another hundred years before serious efforts were made to send Christian missionaries into Arctic and sub-Arctic regions. Anglican missionary societies from England took this initiative. The Church Missionary Society was a prime mover, later assisted by the Bible Churchman's Missionary Society and the Continental and Colonial Missionary Society. The latter sponsored ordinands for Emmanuel College, Saskatoon, Saskatchewan. These young graduates went out to serve in mission areas of the West and North.

Before the end of the nineteenth century, a dozen mission stations had been established throughout both eastern and western Arctic regions. However, the central Arctic area was the last to awaken any serious interest.

What did eventually attract worldwide attention was a report that an unusual band of Eskimos had been found in the central Arctic. These were said to have a distinct resemblance to Europeans, having "blue" eyes. Could it be that they were "blond" Eskimos, descendents of the long-lost Norse settlers? Could they be descendents of the men of the lost Franklin expedition?

This theory did not stand the scrutiny of contemporary science but it did generate excitement and, of course, presented another challenge for Christian missions.

All this took place before the First World War. For several decades before the War, missionaries from the Church of England worked to establish missions in the Arctic. With equal determination, so did the Roman Catholic missionaries from a French order, the Oblates of Mary Immaculate. Each group had a special interest in the Copper Inuit, blonde or not!

As early as l910, the coastal Copper Inuit were visiting Great Bear Lake to trade with D'Arcy Arden, a white trader established there. Hearing of these different coastal people, the Roman Catholic Bishop Breynard sent a priest, Jean-Baptiste Rouviere, to contact them. It seems that, despite language difficulties, a cordial relationship was established. Later, Rouviere was joined by Father Guillaume Leroux, who had some knowledge of the Mackenzie Eskimo dialect.

Intending to visit the coastal camps, the two left their cabin north of Great Bear Lake in the fall of 1913, and eventually arrived at the mouth of the Coppermine River. An Inuk by the name of Hupuk, when interviewed later, stated that the two priests said they were making a short trip then but would return later by ship with supplies. He added that they did not wear skins but long black coats that buttoned to their boots. It was to be a journey from which they would never return.

Eight families who were returning to their camps by dogteam had accompanied them to the coast. The two priests had only two dogs to pull their toboggan, and had no tent. Nothing more was heard from the two priests. When months elapsed without contact, the Church and the RCMP looked into the matter.

Rouviere's diary was found later by the police at the site of the killings, near Bloody Falls on the Coppermine. The last entry in the weather-beaten diary read, "We have arrived at the mouth of the Coppermine. Some families have already gone. Disenchanted with the Eskimo. We have little to eat and don't know what to do."

After considerable investigation, the police worked out a possible scenario.

The priests' possessions, especially the rifles, aroused great interest among the local people who were travelling with them. They were attempting to return to their cabin in the south, but were ill and weak, and their dogs were poorly conditioned and also weak. They lacked a tent, so had little protection from the autumn gales. It is quite likely that they welcomed the arrival of two potential helpers, Ulukhak and Hinikhiak. A confrontation followed, and the priests were left dead in the snow whilst the killers departed with the spoils.

When the police investigated, Ulukhak and Hinikhiak were discovered to have the rifles and the priests' robes in their possession. They were charged with murder. At their court appearance in Calgary, some four years later, they spoke of being yelled at and threatened by the two priests. The victims could not speak for themselves, but the fact that Ulukhak and Hinikhiak had kept the robes and rifles told its own story, and they were found guilty of murder and sentenced to death. They had little understanding of the implications of the sentence and spent extended time in the south as the court system tried to deal with the case.

In the end, their death sentences were commuted and the two were eventually returned to Coppermine, where Ulukhak later died of tuberculosis. The story of Ulukhak and Hinikhiak is well documented in *British Law and Arctic Men*, by R.G. Moyles (1979). In the book, the names are spelled Uluksuk and Sinnisiak, simply variations of the phonetic renderings of names.

Chapter 12

"The Going" from the West

By 1911, news of the "blond Eskimo" had reached the Western Arctic, which by that time had a well-established Anglican presence. This added impetus to the plans already underway to place missionaries in the Central Arctic.

The Anglican Diocese had no knowledge of the intention of the Roman Catholic Church to establish a mission from the Great Bear Lake area, and was already developing plans to move into the Central Arctic by sea during the coming summer.

In the summer of 1912, Reverend W.H. Fry and a small band of Christian natives sailed east from the mouth of the Mackenzie River in the schooner, *Tiliyak*. Unlike the Roman Catholic thrust a year

ABOVE: Springtime camp en route to the Arctic coast from inland.

later, the Anglican party met with no violence. They essentially did not encounter any people, due to poor weather and rough sea conditions. Their mission was aborted for the time being.

Three years later, Bishop Lucas commissioned another attempt under the leadership of the Reverend Herbert Girling. Laymen W.H.B. Hoare, G.F. Merritt, and an Alaskan native called Pauchina, accompanied him. Their vessel bore the name *Atkun*, meaning the "Lightbearer". They were able to reach further east along the coast of the mainland than Fry did in 1912, but experienced a powerful storm which beached them and forced the building of a shelter ashore.

Then, during the unloading of the *Atkun*, something caused the fuel tank to explode, starting a fire that burned the vessel down to the hull. Luckily, none of the travellers was aboard. If they had been on the ship, they could easily have perished. However, they lost most of their food, equipment, and ammunition.

They were forced to live in the makeshift shelter built during the storm, and named it "Camp Necessity". Conditions were primitive, and life was hard indeed. Food supplies were limited, and they were constantly hungry. Of the ten dogs taken along, only three survived.

Finally, on October 1, 1915, Girling and Pauchina set out for the east with their three remaining dogs. After eight days of difficult travel they saw the first camp, the objective of all their efforts. In his journal, Girling expresses his emotions:

"At last the long sought for people were before us. It is customary upon approaching to give the following signs of friendly intent:

"First, the hunting knife is held horizontally at arm's length above the head. Then knees are bent forward until a sitting posture is adopted. The crouching and straightening postures are repeated a few times; all to demonstrate that no weapons are hidden within one's clothing.

But upon this occasion, we reached the tents almost unobserved, and were spared this kind of performance. Upon entering, we called out, "Ilaganaitugut!" ("We are friendly!"), and, immediately, uproarious cries of approval followed. Any attempt to describe my feelings would be inadequate; one's soul rose in thankfulness to God. The past experiences, beaching, loss of the schooner and storms... all forgotten, for here before us were the people who, for three years or more, our Church had striven to reach. The first part of our great task was completed, but the greater part had just now only begun."

For the following four years, Girling and his colleagues made numerous dogteam journeys throughout the Kitengmiut region and met with wide acceptance of their Christian message. Western native believers accompanied them, and undoubtedly assisted with communications and witnessing to the people of the camps. The people had gradually become more familiar with members of the Canadian Arctic Expedition, and had lost much of their suspicion and misunderstanding of strangers. So the mission team was spared any likelihood of the kind of disaster that befell the Roman Catholic enterprise a few years earlier.

In l920, Herbert Girling departed for a furlough and eventually reached Ottawa, where he spoke widely of his experiences. Sadly, he contracted pneumonia and died shortly afterwards.

Many years of consolidation of the Christian mission had been undertaken by the time I arrived in Coppermine in l950. Canon Harold Webster had served for twenty-two years in the area. Practically alone, he had shepherded an Anglican flock extending from Coppermine, north onto Victoria Island, south into the Barrenlands, and east as far as Spence Bay on the Boothia Peninsula.

I learned that serving these congregations, scattered in widely separated hunting camps, involved dogteam travel amounting to some three thousand miles a year (Webster carefully logged every mile!). The parishes east of Cambridge Bay were briefly visited each summer by clergy who travelled on the supply ship.

Initially, Webster and I were the only ordained Anglican clergy-men along some fifteen hundred miles of mainland coastline, between Tuktoyaktuk in the west and Iglulik (Igloolik) in the east. Happily, in later years more recruits allowed for the establishment of new parishes. In the fifties, the Roman Catholic Oblates had remarkable success in developing their missions. In our own expanded parish of Coppermine, there were eight Oblate priests at work despite the fact that the vast majority of the people had already found a spiritual home in the Anglican Church.

What of the relationship between the two denominations - Roman Catholic and Anglican?

In bygone years, stories circulated about the "battle for souls" of the bewildered natives by the two churches. Some were exaggerat-ed, others more factual. From medieval times, ecclesiastical histo-ries are replete with stories of intolerance and even shameful behaviour in many areas of the world. In the service of both Churches in the Arctic, each missionary obviously brought a per-sonal commitment to proclaim the Gospel, as they understood it. Whatever denominational differences there were in presentation, the central Christian message was proclaimed and the people responded according to their own judgment and understanding.

But, the two churches certainly had different philosophies. The Roman Catholic Church traditionally placed strong emphasis on frequent celebrations of the Mass, and thus encouraged their followers to live close to the Mission.

On the other hand, the Anglican faith had deep roots in the evangelistic tradition, and placed great emphasis on the ministry of the Word to the people, wherever they might be. The Diocese encouraged its clergy to travel to the small camps where the people spent their winters. These camps were scattered throughout the Central Arctic in locations that changed in response to the availability of game.

The result was that, in the fifties, we Anglican missionaries spent all the winter months travelling from camp to camp to offer our ministry. We needed the assistance of skilled hunters who guided us to the camps. In each camp, lay leaders were appointed to lead in Christian worship between clergy visits, which might only occur once a year. This helped us to develop a ministry of laymen and encouraged the growth of local leadership in the churches.

In later years, most people moved in off the vast expanse of the land, and the population became concentrated in communities more like those that exist in the south. Today, only a few people still live on the land in small outpost camps, and even these tend to spend a fair amount of their time within the larger communities.

Even considering the differing approaches to Christian ministry between the Roman Catholic and Anglican Churches in these isolated Arctic communities, mutual humanitarian and Christian interests rightly had their place. During our years in Coppermine, every effort was made to maintain good relations with the Roman Catholic missionaries. Opportunities for cooperation on practical levels were always possible. On one occasion, the windcharger belonging to the Roman Catholic mission in the Victoria Island community of Holman broke down. They had no way of charging their batteries to supply electricity for their lights. With only two planes a year, it appeared that, for them, the dark days of winter were going to be somewhat darker.

A rather heavy unit required to repair the windcharger was ordered by radio, and arrived in Coppermine just prior to my long winter journey to the north. There was no question about it - we simply added this item (together with several full mail bags for Holman), to the load on our sled for the seven hundred mile trip (not as the crow flies) to that settlement.

Upon my arrival, Fathers Tardy and Metayer welcomed me graciously and gratefully, supplying me with quantities of seal meat for our dogs. Had I been in their position, they would have done the same for me.

The same feeling exists today. In the present climate of warmth and greater understanding of what essential truths Christians have in common, any spirit of antagonism and suspicion is patently out of place.

Chapter 13

Winter's A'Coming

When autumn comes to the Arctic Coast, the willows turn yellow, the bearberry goes scarlet, and the birches become a lovely salmon colour, all before the end of August. Cranberries shine like jewels, and plump blueberries can be found nestled close to the ground. The grasses set seed and dry up, whispering in the wind. By September, the tundra is bronze-coloured, and long V's of geese pass overhead, honking their way south to their wintering grounds.

By mid-September, the average temperature drops well below freezing, and the Coppermine River begins to freeze, with thin sheets of ice forming in the calmer spots and stretching out from the shore. The nights are dark, and the aurora flickers overhead.

ABOVE: Smooth going, letting the dogs do the pulling! Jack Unipkak and family.

Early fall is an intensely busy time. Building materials come on the sealift, and the main framing-in of any new buildings must be done between the sealift and mid September. Once snow begins to accumulate, outdoor building is difficult. ("Sealift" refers to the conveying of cargo for the settlement by ship.)

In 1950, by the time our new church building was closed in, winter had arrived. This "closing in" of a building in the Arctic is vital. After the outside structure is sealed against the weather, it can be heated and work can continue in relative comfort on the inside.

In those days, there were other tasks that also had to be done in fall. Dog harnesses needed to be repaired and readied for use. Hunters spent a lot of time going over their long adliaks (sleds), fixing lashings, replacing broken crosspieces and the ropes or thongs that hold the load in place. Even today, sled crosspieces are always lashed on the long runners, never nailed or screwed. The lashing allows them to flex as they move over the uneven surface of hard snow, ice, and rocks.

Just after the ice forms on the Coppermine River, there is a predictable run of Arctic char. Everyone sets nets under the ice to gather the harvest. This, too, is still done today, and the timing is important. It is too dangerous to set nets when the ice is too thin. They also cannot easily be set once the ice is more than two feet thick, and the char are also out at sea later, and not accessible in such abundance.

To set a net beneath the newly formed ice involves patiently chipping out a series of holes extending a distance equivalent to the length of the net. Then, a weighted length of cord is lowered in the first hole. A long pole with a hook on the end is angled beneath the ice from the second hole back to the dangling cord. The cord is pulled out the second hole and held in place, weighted end again dangling. The procedure is repeated at the third hole and so on to the end of the series of holes. It is a tedious, and often cold, operation.

Once the cord is in place, the net can be pulled through, from the first hole to the last. It is anchored with long sticks, which are then allowed to freeze into the quickly forming ice. Weights on the bottom of the net allow it to hang suspended in the water, stretched out to effectively snare passing fish as they attempt to swim through the invisible net.

When the net is to be checked (usually each day, as it is best the fish are alive when taken from the net), the new ice in the first and last holes is chipped away and removed. This allows the net and cord to move freely back and forth. The cord remains attached to the net, and is fed into the hole as the net is drawn out the first hole.

Once the catch is removed, the net can easily be reset by pulling it back with the cord.

Setting nets under the ice is not an easy skill to learn, but, once the process is mastered, the results are great fun. It is always exciting to pull the net with its cargo of twisting, wriggling fish from under the ice. Unless they are killed and removed very quickly, they become stiff and frozen into the meshes. If this happens, the net is just returned to the water, where the fish thaw, and the process is repeated.

Most people work barehanded, as the slippery fish are hard to handle with gloves or mitts. Afterwards, your hands ache, but it is a happy ache, as you load your sled with dozens of fat char and tasty whitefish.

When we lived in Coppermine, this early winter run of fish under thin ice was one of the few opportunities to stockpile a staple food for our families and our dogs. Trips were made twice a day to the nets, set some three miles from the community. This afforded opportunities for the dogs to be reintroduced to their harnesses after a summer of idleness. The cooling temperatures, increased food and stimulation usually produced a group of wildly excited dogs. The excitement could make them difficult to handle on the glare ice.

In our part of the Arctic, we carried an anchor attached to the front of the sled by a length of rope. This is an iron "snow hook" about 18 inches long, with two sharp prongs facing down and a handle on top. Theoretically, the dog driver presses it into the snow, bringing the sled to an abrupt halt. In practice, however, this doesn't work quite that well, especially in the fall when one tends to be travelling on a thin layer of snow or on glare ice. In these cases, the hook just bounces along, and the dogs proceed merrily on their way.

I learned this the hard way. On our third trip out for the season in 1950, we started back from the nets with a sled full of fish. The river current had kept ice from forming along a stretch of water between the nets and home, producing an area of open water about the size of a large pond.

Our leader, Snowball, was getting on in years, and was always keen to get home. We loaded up, Webster and I jumped on the sled, and we left the fishing spot at a dead run. Snowball made straight for the open water. We yelled, and used the anchor, but it skittered along the surface of the ice, and the dogs kept going. At the last second, we abandoned ship, and Snowball plunged into the water, followed by the remaining six dogs.

The chill convinced him to take to the ice again, and he and the rest climbed out. Amazingly, the sled followed without tipping, and no one seemed the worse for the experience. Snowball didn't last the winter (his death was unrelated to his dunking), but his fame of taking our precious load of fish home in one piece lived on long after he was gone.

Once the river ice had frozen to a depth of about twelve inches, everyone in the community began to work on getting their winter's water supply from the fresh water ice in the river. Each family needed about two hundred blocks of ice for the winter. One block supplied water for a day. It fitted nicely into a 45-gallon drum in the kitchen, where it was allowed to melt to produce our water for drinking and cooking. But first, one had to get the ice...

To do this, one chopped a basic hole with an ice chisel (we had no power ice augers in 1950), and then used a long ice-saw to cut lengths of ice. The correct size of blocks of ice were then chipped out with an ice-fork, and hoisted out onto the solid ice with ice tongs. Each block weighed about 35 pounds.

Because the river ice was new and had not yet reached its midwinter thickness, there were often dangerous cracks, hidden by the snow. This could lead to accidents.

On one occasion, in the early sixties, I was chipping away, releasing a block from two converging cuts I had already made. I did not know I was standing on an unseen fissure. There was a loud "Craack!" and down I went with a splash, into the open water.

The shock of the cold was incredible, and I understood why, years earlier, Snowball had shot out of the water as quickly as he did.

I thrust my wet mitts onto solid ice, where they immediately froze, preventing me from being carried under the ice by the current. This also provided leverage by which I could climb out, somewhat slower than Snowball did.

My young assistant, Christopher Williams, was with me. Once it was clear that I would survive, and he would not have to conduct his first Arctic funeral, he (and everyone else) seemed to find all this quite amusing.

By the time I had walked the fifty yards or so to the mission house, my clothing had frozen solid and was like stiff cardboard. I was deeply thankful I did not have miles to go to a warm haven.

When this ice-sheathed apparition, festooned with icicles, staggered into our kitchen, a rather surprised mission wife was at a loss for words. My teeth were chattering so hard I was unable to explain what had happened. However, once I'd warmed up and changed to dry clothing, she heard the story. As the ice-cutting operation was not complete, back I went, wiser for the experience. Betty watched with some anxiety from the house.

When the oblong of open water had surrendered its frozen contents, we roped it off and lit a lantern there each night to prevent other folks from taking an unforeseen dip in the river. Once the new ice in the opening was about 3 inches thick, the whole procedure began again.

This time, we cut pieces the size of pavement slabs, clear ice that was much lighter to handle. These were also hauled up to the mission, and used to construct ice porches for the house and the church.

Porches are important in the Arctic, as they provide protection from the incessant winds and keep snow from blowing in around a door. In those early days, wood was in short supply, and many buildings lacked porches or entryways. Even if a building had an entryway, an ice porch was often built to provide a convenient storage place for winter gear and food. Ice was not in short supply, and functioned admirably as a building material.

The slabs of ice were used as building blocks, and were cemented together with a "mortar" consisting of a slush of snow and water slapped onto each row of slabs, and between each adjoining slab. Tarpaulins were used to roof these ice porches.

When winter winds howled around the house, it was amazing how protective the ice porch proved to be. One stepped "outside" into stillness, freezing cold, but without the cutting wind.

Our good friends and neighbours, the Munros, from the Hudson's Bay Company also built an ice porch each year. Bill and I had a fierce competition to see who could erect the more impressive structure in the shortest possible time. Ours was quite functional, containing a "larder" with shelves stocked with fat char, caribou, and home-baked bread. We found that taking fresh loaves straight from the oven to the porch, allowed them to quick-freeze without gradual cooling. When loaves treated this way were brought inside and thawed, they tasted fresh-baked.

Later, after more snow had fallen and was packed by the wind into hard banks, we completely surrounded our houses with snow walls. Snow is a superb insulator, and helped keep out the wind. We cut snow blocks similar to those used in iglu-building, and banked the entire house, up to the level of the windows. This allowed us to keep the house much warmer while using much less coal (which was our fuel in the early 50s) or, later, fuel oil.

From all of this, it is apparent that the onset of winter was a very busy time in the small settlement of Coppermine. Winter preparations where people lived in houses were regarded with some amusement by many of our parishioners who lived in small camps out on the land. They were much more skilled at using snow, and followed a much simpler procedure — building entire houses (iglus) of it (in the northern parts of our region) or banking caribou skin tents with snow blocks in the southern inland camps.

As primitive as it seemed, we valued that little mission house. It had been built in 1929, when the first Christian mission was established in Coppermine. Its walls were insulated, but the floors were not. This produced a great variation in temperature indoors, from cosy warmth at head level to freezing cold along the floor. Betty and I always wore caribou skin boots (*kamiks*) in the winter, and our children, particularly in their early crawling days, were similarly protected.

Once there was enough snow to partially envelop our house, our cooking stove and space heaters kept us warm enough. Before a community generating plant was built, our electricity was provided by a "windcharger", a windmill contraption that energized a modest bank of batteries. This gave us light from low wattage bulbs. When the wind did not blow, we used gasoline or kerosene lamps.

For six weeks in December and January, the sun did not rise above the southern horizon, creating a sort of twilight for about four hours at mid-day. There was so much to do during those six weeks that the time seemed to pass very quickly.

Although few families actually lived in the settlement at that time, visitors were frequent. Families from nearby camps constantly came and went, stopping in to share stories and news. In general, settlement life was good, with a healthy sense of community and mutual kindness.

For me, the comfort of home in the mission house was treasured, a welcome prospect in a mission which demanded weeks of absence and a strenuous life on the trail each winter.

Chapter 14

Dark Days, Bright Prospects

In the fall, the days rapidly shorten until in early November the sun vanishes below the southern horizon, not to appear again until late in January.

In winter, true darkness at noon occurs only in the very high latitudes. During the month of December, Coppermine experiences a bright twilight from about 10:30 AM until 2 PM. The light is such that one could easily work outdoors, but it does not last long. However, on clear starlit evenings, or during a full moon, travel and other activities are possible at night. The snow-covered land reflects the meagre light, making it appear much brighter than in the south.

When we lived in Coppermine, one blessing of the dark days of

ABOVE: May Agliyuituk bringing more blubber into the snowhouse.
Photo: Canon Harold Webster.

winter was a great improvement of radio reception from southern Canada. During the spring and summer months, we were able to receive short-wave stations from all over the world. There seemed to be no limit. The BBC boomed in twenty-four hours a day, and we frequently could hear broadcasts from as far away as central Africa.

Stations in southern Canada, on the other hand, were silent. But the Soviet Union boomed in year round, extolling the virtues of the communist system. In summer, this became quite frustrating. I once wrote a rather facetious letter to the CBC, complaining about their neglect of the North, and stating that each summer the only sports news we heard were those of Soviet athletic prowess, to the point that our children were reduced to singing our national anthem to the tune of The Volga Boatman! Just a few months later, CBC North came on the air, and has continued to broadcast ever since.

Winter truly was welcome in this country. Snow and ice were viewed as gifts and blessings. Insect pests vanished, and travel, housing, and many other aspects of life became easier in winter. Lakes and the sea became a highway, not a barrier, and the coating of snow on the ground made travel by dogteam possible, usually by November. However, we could not travel to the winter camps of many of our parishioners until after Christmas, when the frozen ocean became a highway. Together, the snowy land, ocean, and lakes allowed travel in any direction, beneficial in a land where railroads and asphalt roads were not only impossible, but also unnecessary.

Housing also became easier. Most of our people moved from canvas or caribou skin tents into snowhouses in December, when enough wind-packed snow was available for building. The building materials were free, allowed for construction to suit every family, and, if you wanted to move to another location, you just built another snowhouse. No building permits were necessary.

Snow assisted the hunters as well — the snow was a living map of all who passed over it. Animals left tracks that directed hunters to the best places to intercept their prey.

Winter even made communication easier. The isolation of the summer camps was over, snow and ice allowed people to return to the coastal areas in time to join us for the great festival of Christmas.

In 1950, I looked forward with great anticipation to meeting a small group of people living inland, but only one day's journey from the coast. The vast majority of "*Nunamiut*" (people of the land) lived far inland, many days' travel to the south.

Our destination was a two-roomed snowhouse - just two domed

rooms jutting off at right angles from a common porch or entrance dome. An old couple (Aivgak and Uliguna) with a son in his forties occupied one section, whilst their daughter, her husband, and two children occupied the other.

As a newcomer, I was referred to as the *kavlunak* (or white man). Once we *kavlunait* were known and accepted, we Anglican missionaries became the *minihitait* — the closest they could get to "minister". The Roman Catholic priests were *fallas* (from "Father"). So changed the language, with more and more English terms creeping in.

A brief aside, in explanation, here: changes have accelerated in recent years as orthography and linguistics have been applied to the language as a whole. There are two distinct sounds, which are technically identified by either a "k" or a "q".

Important as it is for a learner to know which is the correct sound, to the people themselves, the concern is small. This can be compared to the "confusion" that might occur in the minds of English-speaking people with words such as "school"; it may be more sensible to replace the "sch" with "sk", but it isn't done, and doesn't bother those used to the language.

Most of the elders still prefer the "k" method of writing, and, out of respect to them, I have in this book retained the older method of spelling.

Over time, I had managed some study of Inuinaktun and had a modest vocabulary.... but these people didn't seem to use the words I had learned! Also, they spoke at great speed, and I just could not follow them. I could read the service book, and that was about all.

To break the "sound barrier", so to speak, became a major goal. It was going to take a few years before I was at home in the language, able to appreciate the humour and communicate freely. Expectations were high — the people wanted their minister to be not only a teacher and dispenser of the Word and Sacrament, but also to be a storyteller, a sharer of news, and a confidante, capable of hearing and understanding the deepest of social and personal problems. All that was a long way away for me.

My main memory of that visit in 1950 was a strange feeling of enforced silence, common to all newcomers who do not really KNOW the language of the land.

On the first day out, we met up with a hunter, Alfred Okkaituk, who later became a close friend and travelling companion. Alfred and a young relative were hunting caribou on the Coppermine River, and stopped to share a cup of tea with us. We had shot four caribou, which the hunters helped me learn how to skin, and we headed home with the fresh meat.

Okkaituk and the lad were less fortunate. After we left, they were hunting at the top of a ridge. Alfred had jammed his sled anchor into the snow, and had a caribou in his sights. His first shot wounded it, and off it went in a speedy, but injured, condition. When the dogs smelled the blood, they sprang into action, dragging the anchor out, and pursued the caribou. The hunters gave chase, but were quickly left behind. The ridge gave way to a steep cliff, and the caribou went over the edge, followed by the dogs and the sled. All the dogs were killed in the fall, crushed to death at the bottom of the cliff. In the space of a few seconds, Alfred became impoverished.

His return was greeted with much sympathy. Different families, our own included, gave him dogs to replace his team. Of course, these were not all their best dogs, and it took some time for Okkaituk to become really established again.

When he was an older man, Alfred told me that, as a small boy, he went with his parents to trade at Great Bear Lake. He said that two priests (Fathers Le Roux and Rouviere, mentioned earlier) were there, and one laid his hand on his head, and stated that he hoped the boy would one day become a Christian leader. With a typical turn of humour, Alfred said to me, "Well, I have become a Christian leader, but the priest did not say in which Church!"

Chapter 15

Travelling Times

Well before the end of 1950, the "missionary-in-charge" (as Canon Webster was officially designated) informed me of the annual travelling routine for St. Andrew's Mission. It was impressive — some 3000 miles each year, all by dogsled.

Anglican missionaries travelled out to the camps of the people within their region. Many of these families seldom visited the trading posts established several years earlier. When they did visit, celebrations, trading, and visits with friends took up so much of the day that there was little time or opportunity left for much Christian teaching. In addition, many trading posts were without a resident Anglican missionary. We needed to

ABOVE: Leaving on a long journey. Photo: Canon Harold Webster.

make personal visits to each camp.

Our annual trips would begin with a visit to a settlement on the southwestern coast of Victoria Island, called Read Island. People had gathered there for Christmas, and would be staying there for the New Year's celebrations. Travel to Read Island would take a week each way.

Once we were back, and had rested the dogs, then we would make a trip south to several inland camps. This would take about three weeks.

Before the end of February, we would make an extended trip to western Victoria Island, over a long portage to Prince Albert Sound to another Hudson's Bay Company post and Roman Catholic Mission at Holman Island. From there, we would head north to camps on Minto Inlet, just to the east of Banks Island. This trip would last six weeks and cover fourteen hundred miles.

Finally, as the days became longer in the spring, we would head east to Cambridge Bay on the southeast coast of Victoria Island, then turn south to visit camps around Bathurst Inlet before making for home.

Apart from breaks at home, mostly to renew our supplies and rest our dogs, our team was on the move or preparing for the next trip from December until late June or July.

Realizing the heavy responsibilities of the single mission covering such a large geographic area, the Bishop felt Webster needed an assistant. Also, the Webster family was soon to move to a mission in the Mackenzie Delta. I would have to take over this ambitious travelling plan.

Luckily, I was to be "broken in" in stages! I must admit the analogy of a sled dog briefly crossed my mind as Webster told me this....

During my first visit to an inland camp, described earlier, I was in the hands of Jack Allonak. Jack had learned English while attending the Anglican residential school in Aklavik, some years earlier. It was on that trip that I learned how utterly dependent one becomes in a totally different culture and environment. Despite all the years before without any kind of sheltered upbringing, the challenges of life in the wartime Royal Navy, and the challenges of theological education, I had never experienced such a sense of helplessness. The Arctic environment reduced one to the state of an infant just starting life. The secret was to accept just how ignorant one was, to be constantly teachable, ever ready to laugh at yourself...and never, EVER lose one's temper, whatever happens. Over many years, as I listened to the people speaking of the early missionaries, I found the ones held in highest regard were those who, in the worst possible situations, especially on the trail, remained calm without lambasting their guides and fellow travellers.

Harold Webster was a responsible teacher. He did all he could to share his experiences with me in order that I would be prepared to avoid serious mishaps, teaching me as much as possible about survival in this harsh and unforgiving land.

And, he made sure I was correctly outfitted. Well before Christmas, I had to be completely fitted for travel, in the best of traditional caribou skin clothing. In Coppermine, unlike many other Eastern Arctic settlements, we had a reliable supply of caribou skins suitable for clothing. Once the lakes froze and snow covered the land, creating favourable travel conditions, the Inlanders returned to the coast, bringing fall caribou skins for trade. These were best for use in clothing.

My outfit was tailored for me by local women, and consisted of several layers of caribou skin with the hair left on the skin. Next to the body, I had a hooded *atigi* of caribou skin with the hair inside, and inner pants of fur. The hood on this inner garment had a ruff of wolverine. Wolverine fur is used because the frost that builds up on it from your breath does not stick, and freely falls off, avoiding the annoyance of ice around your face. My outer *kulitak* (parka) was made of caribou skin with the hair outside, and a closely fitted hood with a ruff of wolf fur. On my feet, I wore caribou socks with the hair inside, and over these, *kamiks* (boots) made from the leg skins of the caribou, with soles of more durable moosehide. Caribou skin mitts protected my hands. When I was dressed in all this, I had all the agility of a medieval knight in full armour. But I was warm.

Canon Webster told me of a 1931 trip he made alone in February, which is our coldest month. It was a short trip, and he was not far from home when the weather turned stormy. His lead dog slipped its harness and ran off. Webster made the mistake of leaving his sled and trying to follow the dog's tracks to catch it. Soon drifting snow covered both his tracks and the dog's. He could see nothing, and apparently walked in circles. Completely lost, he hunched up each night in a snowbank. He had no food, and no way to start a fire. Four days later, after his team found its way home, and a search was started, he was found and taken home. Despite all the cold and wind, his skin clothing protected every limb and digit; he was not frostbitten at all. I listened with great respect, and never forgot the lessons he taught me.

For me, personally, by always travelling with experienced "men of the land", dramatic and dangerous situations were avoided. We were many times temporarily lost in blizzards, but simply camped and found our way again once the weather cleared.

Sometimes, we had slight difficulty finding a camp. The people may have moved their seal hunting camp to a different location in order to find more seals, but they always left tracks we could follow. In really bad weather, the dogs could still find the camp if it was upwind, as they caught the scent miles before we could see any sign of camp.

Of course, situations differ widely. One spring, Alfred Okkaituk and I were returning from Victoria Island in comparatively warm weather. The snow was getting soft and "punchy", and we were advised to get home quickly, before sled travel became impossible. To accomplish this, we had to make a portage across a large peninsula after crossing the sea ice on Dolphin and Union Straits.

In the springtime, it is far better to travel at night as the temperatures are lower then, and travel is easier when the snow hardens. We followed this practice for two nights. On the third day, as we slept, the sun shone strongly, too strongly! We woke, and peered through the tent flap, and recoiled in shock. Most of the snow had melted, and the brown of the tundra peeped through the snow for miles around.

We commenced a wearisome struggle, zig-zagging from snowdrift to snowdrift, and dragging the sled over the bare patches of tundra. But, we had an unexpected ally that spring. Lemmings were at the peak of their cycle, and they were everywhere. There were lemmings running madly about, dashing ahead of the dogs, diving into their tunnels, wriggling enticingly, and, for the dogs, deliciously.

Our dogs were delighted. They lunged one way, then another, snapping up furry mouthfuls with glee. Their incessant "hunting" at least kept us moving, mostly in the correct direction.

Thinking our little girl, Angela, would be thrilled to have a few of these furry creatures for pets, we managed to rescue four from the mouths of the dogs, and packed them into a biscuit box on the sled.

Once we had completed the portage and were again on the sea ice, we made our way home, still with scores of lemmings milling around on the sea ice, but the going improved considerably. We were making about three miles an hour.

On the last stretch, close to Coppermine, we waded knee-deep through overflow on the river ice before being greeted on the shore by our families and anxious friends.

We arrived at the mission house, unharnessed the weary dogs, and presented our trophies to the welcoming family. Betty's response might have been foreseen, she cried, "What on earth are these for? We have hundreds running around outside the house, and can't use any more!" She had apparently been battling a mouse invasion for days during our absence.

So we "studied" them briefly (Angela was delighted, by the way), and released them to join their compatriots scurrying about the mission. I was glad I had not bothered to gift wrap my present!

Chapter 16

Kuviahugvik – Christmas

Before the coming of the explorers, traders, and missionaries, the period of the year that is the darkest, together with weeks of bitterest cold, would never have been referred to as *kuviahugvik* or "a time of happiness." In former times, people came together for drum dances and celebrations during the bright days of spring, when the promise of summer became apparent, just before departing for their nomadic inland wanderings. Late December found all the Kitengmiut scattered over the frozen ocean at seal hunting camps. Here they sought the breathing holes of ringed and bearded seals, at that time of year their only source of life - meat for the body and oil for the soapstone lamps.

ABOVE: Ikey Bolt and young friend.

But the explorers, traders and missionaries introduced the idea of a midwinter festival - Christmas. Of course, for the missionaries, it was a time to tell the story of the birth of the Son of God. For the most secular of traders and explorers, it was a timely reason for a joyous relief from the dark dreariness of an Arctic winter.

By the time our family lived on the Arctic coast, the Christmas season had become a treasured time in the North. After the coming of the trading posts, the annual lives of the people revolved around running traplines and trading for goods of all sorts. Trapping did not usually commence until the white fox furs were "prime", fully white and very thick, about early November on the coast. The first trading trip to the post occurred around Christmas.

Also, people who had spent the summer hunting caribou on the inland lakes and rivers usually returned to the settlement in December, sleds piled high with skins. Coppermine usually increased its population by some three hundred percent at this time. Hundreds of dogs were tethered along the shoreline, adding to the chaos by greeting each incoming team with a chorus of howling. It is a time of great excitement. Everyone must shake hands, even the smallest children. Babies poke their heads from their mothers' atigis for a kiss. Dogs are unharnessed and staked out on lines so they cannot fight. Calls for tea echo all over the place. Iglus are built along the shore on the sea ice.

Our Christmas preparations actually began at shiptime in September. The yearly ship delivered numerous bales of clothing and gifts from many Anglican Women's Auxiliaries in the south, all addressed to "St. Andrew's Mission, Coppermine." These were the annual gifts of ladies' groups in the south, the Anglican Women's Auxiliary, who spent much time collecting and preparing clothing for northern missions. Boxes of toys came from the Holy Trinity Churches in Edmonton and Yellowknife. These were stashed away, unopened, until the big event.

The enormous contribution of the missionary-minded ladies in so many churches in the south earned the gratitude of many of us in those years. We sorted and resorted the clothing, making sure each man, woman, and child had something. Then we sorted the toys and tagged them with the names of recipients.

Often, the Coronation Gulf was not frozen enough to permit travel from Victoria Island across to the mainland. So our Christmas gatherings usually included people from the camps along the coast and inland families from no great distance. We always knew whom to expect, and this was taken into consideration in marking gifts. Opening bales and boxes occupied about a week of our time. Not all gifts were suitable, but, somehow before "The Day", a gift was found for each person, and each child had a toy. For so many, that present was the only gift they would receive all year.

Especially prized were discarded fur coats from the south. Some were from fur-bearing animals unknown in the north, like minks and raccoons. These were often given to older folk, mainly because, unlike caribou, they did not shed their hair. These were often turned inside out and made into long lasting *atigis* (local term for "parkas"). Even artificial fur coats were eagerly received and converted to atigis.

Some of our customs of Christmas decoration were not at first understood. The story is told of a Hudson's Bay Company trader, who sent his native assistant off on a dogsled trip to the treeline with orders to bring him a tree for Christmas. The assistant evidently found a tree of some stature, one that might have been suitable. But, in order to more easily transport it on his sled, he cut off all the branches and carefully lashed the trunk to the sled. One can only imagine the trader's reaction, and hope he was a man of humour.

In the Mission, we prepared for Christmas. We were to feed everyone after the morning service on Christmas Day. To feed upwards of two hundred people required energy, imagination, strength, and stamina.

We had a large dog-pot, usually used to give our dogteam an occasional warm meal of commercial feed. This was scoured out and filled with a large quantity of cooked rice into which raisins were mixed.

One would think that the people would like a change from their daily diet of raw frozen fish, but no, they liked the fish. Dozens of Arctic char were slightly thawed and sliced into cutlets. There were piles of caribou meat, also partially thawed and ready to be cut up with ulus and eaten. By the end of the feast, only scraps were left.

Betty spent days up to her elbows in flour, making scores of scones. For dessert, there was stewed dried fruit. It was all washed down with gallons of tea.

It is the Christmas services that evoke the most poignant memories for me.... Christmas Eve was always special in the modest mission church, so full of the joys of the season. Sometimes we were blessed with a still starlit night with the silence only broken by an occasional howling chorus from the hundreds of sled dogs that surrounded the settlement.

People crowded into the church, hearing the ancient story and the proclamations of the angels, and singing praise of the Lord Jesus who came so long ago at this season.

PREVIOUS PAGE: Fred Kahak
having tea on the trail, on Prince
Albert Sound, Victoria Island.

ABOVE: June, a Kahak family
member, having tea on a bitterly
cold day, Prince Albert Sound.

RIGHT: Martha Kukiyayuk in
beautiful caribou clothing, having
a "mug-up" of tea on the trail to
Concession Lake, inland from
Coppermine.

TOP: Sperry serving a treat of rice and raisins at a Christmas feast in Coppermine. Left, Tom Kokak, Middle, Marion Hayokuk.

ABOVE: Christmas pageant at St. Andrew's Mission, 1966. Young John Sperry is the shepherd to the left of "Mary", dressed in a pink tablecloth, but carrying a realistic shepherd's crook.

FAR LEFT: Fur-clad missionary.

ABOVE: Stopping for tea while running a trapline on Prince Albert Sound, Victoria Island. Left, Alec Banksland; right, Sam Oliktoak.

LEFT: Child in caribou clothing (kulitak) with wolverine ruff, pieced caribou trim, and caribou kamiks (boots).

ABOVE: Teatime on the trail.
Winnie Tupitak, James Hala,
Connie Nalvana, Sperry, and
Martha Kukiyayuk and
Hala's son.

LEFT: Small child at church
service, dressed in calico atigi
(parka) with a fox ruff.

TOP: Sam Oliktoak driving the mission team on the Coronation Gulf near Richardson Island.

ABOVE: White fox skins hanging to dry before being bundled to take to a trading post. Photographer unknown.

ABOVE: Jack Allonak icing runners on qamutiik (sled) on the trail to Bathurst Inlet.

RIGHT: The coming of the thermos bottle made life much easier, as hot drinks could be carried on the sled and served out quickly. Here Jack Allonak serves tea on a relatively warm day; he would not be able to hold the metal thermos in his bare hands on a cold day!

FAR RIGHT: Sam Oliktoak checking with a telescope for a route through pressure ridges. He is dressed in a caribou kulita and polar bear pants.

ABOVE: Travelling by dogteam was fun when done in a group, as the dogs were much more active and fellowship was delightful, with comments being shouted back and forth.

LEFT: Walter Bolt Wikhak in spring atigi with his Brownie box camera, quite a novelty in those days.

TOP: Pressure ridge on the sea ice off Williams Point, Dolphin and Union Straits. Sam Oliktoak has climbed to the top to try to determine a way through the jumbled ice.

ABOVE: Sam Oliktoak's team on the sea ice of Prince Albert Sound. The leader is a good example of the aboriginal Eskimo dog that accompanied the people across the Bering Land Bridge.

TOP: Trixie and teammate resting from work. Trixie wears a protective blanket to prevent chilling.

ABOVE: Dogs stop to scentmark every little piece of ice along the trail. Here Walter Bolt Wikhak admonishes his

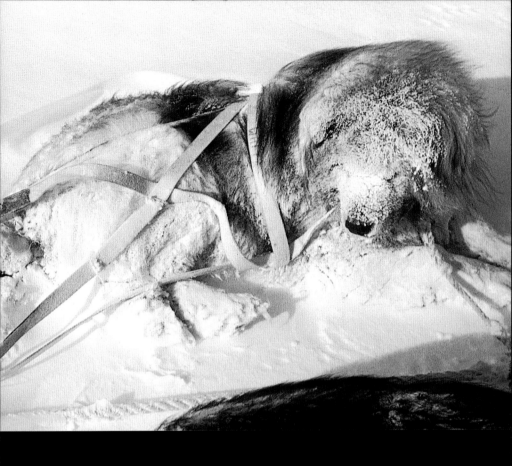

TOP: Storms of short duration did not particularly bother well-fed dogs; they just curl up in the snow on rest stops or at night. Dogs were unharnessed at night, so this is a rest stop.

ABOVE: RCMP Constable Douglas Ferguson clearing ice from a dog's face during a rest stop. Note how quickly drifts form around the dogs in blowing snow.

ABOVE: Jack Allonak hitching his dogs. The singletree type bar across the back of the harness distributes the weight better on the dog's shoulders and chest.

RIGHT: Team hitched and ready to go. Jack Allonak holds a restless dog. This is a good example of the "Nome" hitch or gangline hitch in which the dogs are hitched in pairs.

FAR RIGHT: Typical travel scene. These teams traveled about four miles an hour, and travelers often walked alongside the sled to keep warm and relieve the dogs of weight.

TOP: Holman settlement in the 1950s.
The only permanent buildings (other
than the Roman Catholic Mission
building, not in this photo) were those
of the Hudson's Bay Company post

ABOVE: Adliak (sled) ready for loading
and harnessing of the dogs. The team is
staked away from the harnesses, as many
will chew them. Note the "snow hook" or
sled anchor to left of the sled

All played their parts, our "little angels" together with older "shepherds", and the "holy family" in a still tableau. The "wise men", bedecked with robes and other clothing from the bales and bejewelled with southern trinkets, made their pilgrimage down a very crowded child-strewn aisle to honour the holy child. For a brief time, we were all transported to "Bethlehem of Judea".

Following the joy and solemnity of the Christmas Eve service, all pandemonium broke out. Everyone had to wish everyone else a very "Merry Christmas!" in English. For many, this sounded like "Melly Kolaisimas", but the emotion and the intent was there.

For us the carols sung in the language of the people had all the solemn impact and heart-warming joy of the same familiar carols sung in English. *Silent Night.... O Come All Ye Faithful....* they stir the hearts of people everywhere, no matter the language. At the end of this section of the book, we have included *Silent Night* as an example.

After the service on Christmas Day, the greetings and the feasting, there were games and sled dog races. Teams of seven dogs dashed off to a nearby island and then back to town. The winners emerged grinning and clutching prizes donated by the Hudson's Bay Company. Later, there were square dances in the newly built school. Of course, in those days, all was done without the stimulation of alcohol. Christmas was, indeed, a very blessed, holy, and merry time. Stories of the birth of the Saviour and the Good News of His coming into the world evoked a response of obvious and joyful praise. Among us were lined and marked faces that grew up in an earlier world of fear and uncertainty. No one expressed any objection to the Gospel of Christ having been declared and shared in their part of the frozen world. Without feeling any sense of apology, one felt both humbled and proud for having been called to proclaim it.

SILENT NIGHT, HOLY NIGHT

Unuak naguyuk,	Silent night, holy night,
Talvani nunami,	All is calm, all is bright.
Uilagahuk nutaganikpaktuk	Yonder the Virgin Mother and Child,
Angutinuak ataniuyuk	Holy Infant so tender and mild.
Negiyutikagvingmi-ituk	Sleep in heavenly peace...
Anilihaktuk Jesus.	Sleep in heavenly peace.
Unuak naguyuk,	Silent night, holy night,
Imnailigit hivullit,	Only for the shepherds' sight
Ihalgulgit tautukpagailli	Came blest visions of angel throngs,
Hagyaegmata ukakhutik	With their loud alleluia songs.
Christ Jesus-guk tikitpaktuk	Saying, Christ is come...
Anilihakhunilu.	Saying, Christ is come.
Unuak naguyuk,	Silent night, holy night,
Nutagak kilangmin,	Child of Heaven, O how bright.
Kaiyuk annautiyumavlugit	Thou didst smile on us
Nagligivagamigit inuit	When thou wast born.
Annauyyi tamna inuyuk	Blest indeed was that happy morn,
Annauyikhakpaut Jesus	Full of heavenly joy,
	Full of heavenly joy.

The Inuinaktun version of *Silent Night* was translated by John R. Sperry (1990). The English version used here is from the traditional Anglican hymnal, and is the version from which the Inuinaktun version was translated. The English version was translated by Jane M. Campbell (1863) from the original German version by Reverend Joseph Mohr.

Chapter 17

Fur and Fashions

The harsh Arctic winter makes good clothing a necessity, not a matter of fashion. Being warmly dressed can make the difference between life and death on the land. It is the fur of animals that has made the difference.

The bitter cold cuts like a knife. In the depths of an Arctic winter, at -30º C (-22º F) with a searing wind, unprotected human flesh freezes within 40 seconds. Exposed fingertips become numb upon contact with any metal. You always watch the faces of your travelling companions for white waxy spots. These are signs of frostbite, which must be dealt with rapidly, before the freezing goes deep into the skin. This is done by turning away from the wind, and placing the

ABOVE: Family dressed in the wonderful caribou garments so typical of the 1950s. June Okalik, daughter, and Andy Klengenberg. Photo: Canon Harold Webster.

bare palm of your hand upon the affected spot until colour returns.

I quickly came to appreciate the advice of Harold Webster regarding clothing. His years of experience in the Arctic made him truly an authority. Once winter travelling began, one adapted with what was available in terms of furs and fabrics, mostly furs.

The warmest possible mitts (*pualuk*; plural *pualuit*) are those made of wolf skin. However cold the weather, your hands remain warm, even perspiring, in wolf mitts. Using a light pair of canvas gloves inside the wolf mitts makes tasks like harnessing dogs or lighting a primus stove much easier. Once the job is finished, on go the mitts again.

Caribou skin clothing is the warmest possible option for winter wear in Arctic climates. Recent tests performed in climate-controlled chambers have proven caribou clothing superior to the most high-tech of fabric clothing. Volunteers in the synthetic clothing were shivering far earlier than those in the caribou clothing, at the same temperatures. Add wind, and the synthetic materials fell further behind.

However, any skin clothing quickly shows signs of wear. The hairs of the caribou are filled with large air cells, which improves their insulating qualities, but renders the hairs brittle. They eventually break off, especially in areas of constant friction, such as under the arms, and the clothing loses its ability to insulate. For this reason, a new set of clothing is usually needed at least every three years.

This shedding of hairs also means that caribou hairs get into absolutely everything — especially your tea. During a "mug-up" on the trail, your steaming mug of tea or coffee quickly collects caribou hairs on its surface. A well-directed blast of air over the rim of the mug will disperse most of them. The rest you simply drink, as the prospect of fishing for them with bare fingers in the searing cold is not attractive.

When you eventually get to a trading post where a shower is possible - sometimes delayed for more days or weeks than you wish to remember - caribou hair is more than a memory. One's exposed feet reveal little tufts of caribou hair between each toe, a sort of friendly insulating gesture.

There were different fashions in clothing right across the Arctic. In the Central Arctic, there was an enthusiastic adoption of Alaskan styles, arriving with the Canadian Arctic Expedition of 1913. By the time I lived in the Central Arctic, both men and women had long since abandoned the high-waisted, "swallow tail" pattern of the *atigis* (parkas) their forebears used, in favour of longer and warmer garments.

Before the leghold trap was available, people were forced to capture furbearing animals in stone traps or with snares, both difficult methods that yielded few skins. With the use of the leghold trap and the rifle, a greater variety of fur was available. The use of fur ruffs and trim for the bottom and sleeves of the garment was virtually unknown before the coming of the leghold trap, but became widespread once these were used.

Wolverine fur was used for the inner ruff of the hood. The individual hairs of wolverine fur are quite slick and, as mentioned earlier, the frost from one's breath is easily brushed off. Other fur, such as that of wolf or fox, retains the frost, which becomes clotted and rough on the face and chin.

In the Eastern Arctic, dog or puppy fur is widely used on ruffs, as wolves and wolverines are not common. I have asked our people why they do not use dog fur. One reply was, "It would be like skinning a relative!" This seems a curious response, but one that illustrates the close relationship the people felt with their dogs.

The drive to fulfill the European demand for fur for high fashion launched and sustained the fur trade in Canada, beginning with the need for beaver furs for felt hats. Generally speaking, historic relations with the aboriginal peoples of Canada were based on mutual interests — the local people were as interested in the new goods and technologies as the Europeans were in their furs.

In southern Canada, beaver pelts were the main attraction. In the North, it was the white (Arctic) fox, and other furbearers - the marten and lynx south of the treeline, and the fox, wolf, and musk ox on the tundra.

In the coat of arms of the Northwest Territories (before Division into two territories), the face of a white fox looked out from the red background representing the tundra. This symbolized the historic role of the fur industry in the development of the North.

Before the arrival of the explorers and traders, people laboriously constructed traps for various animals, using solely rocks and boulders. A favourite style for foxes was the beehive-shaped structure with a small hole at the top. The fox climbed up the outside, jumped in to get the bait, and was unable to climb out because of the inwardly-inclining sides.

More complicated styles of stone traps with ground level entrances were used for wolves and wolverines. Some of these had intricately designed vertical sliding stone trapdoors. These were propped up with a thin stick, to which was attached a line. The line ran back through the trap, around a stick thrust through the back of the chamber, and to a fish head or other bait. When the animal tugged on the bait, out came the stick, down came the door, and it was trapped.

Once trappers and traders brought in the leghold trap, the entire way of life of the hunting peoples of the North changed forever.

With the need to service long traplines for fur, larger dogteams were raised. The use of the rifle guaranteed easier hunting for food. The traders encouraged people to spend more time trapping by providing the enticements of new technology, metal cookware, stoves, needles, fabrics, and rifles. The desire for new utensils, clothing, and foodstuffs increased yearly.

From the viewpoint of the local people, this was an enormous benefit. I myself have seen how long it takes to boil a kettle of water on a seal oil lamp compared to boiling it on a primus or gasoline stove. Before the coming of the trade goods, hunters on the trail in winter could only quench their thirst in the most primitive way. They stuffed the gullet of a seal with snow, and suspended it against their naked chests or over their backs under their atigis so that body heat would melt enough water for an occasional drink.

After the coming of the traders, more options were available. A trapper with his fox pelts for trade could buy a thermos bottle, which would keep tea hot for hours, or a primus stove which could provide scalding hot water in a few minutes. Steel needles made life so much easier for many northern women who previously had to sew with sinew and needles of bone or copper.

Modern calls for the "good old days" mainly come from those who have little understanding of what was involved in day to day living in the past. For all the attendant problems that would come with the technologies brought by the trappers and traders, the new possessions made life so much easier. Arrivals from Europe and the south brought new diseases and other serious problems, yes, but so many things they brought were, understandably, very welcome indeed.

The economy in the Arctic was built on trapping and hunting; particularly of seals and white foxes. In recent years, both pursuits have received vigorous, vicious opposition in the south and in Europe. This has literally destroyed the industry, and has reduced a previously independent people, in many cases, to welfare recipients.

One of the blessings of winter is the simple fact that the fur of many animals reaches prime condition only in the coldest months of winter. This fact is often forgotten when anti-trapping lobby groups illustrate torn and bleeding trapped animals in a climate where the pain obviously would be agonizing and cruel. The leghold trap, used in the Arctic cold, inflicted a minimum of pain, as the fox's paw would freeze within minutes. Certainly, it awaited death when the trapper arrived, but this was no different than the death awaiting millions of livestock bred especially for the discriminating palates of southern populations. Despite the often-exaggerated concern about the use of leghold traps, these are now illegal, and have been replaced by the Conibear trap. When sprung by an animal, these instantly kill it without suffering.

The same could be said of those that oppose all hunting of seals. The commercial seal hunts are far different from the Inuit seal hunts. The Inuit hunter takes only a few seals at a time, primarily for their meat and blubber. Little is wasted. Yet anti-seal hunting campaigners lump all hunting of seals together, and have destroyed the market for seal products. Very few of these campaigners are vegetarians or abstainers of using leather, which, of course, is the product of a purposely-slaughtered innocent beast. Small wonder that the people who depend on the harvest of the land and sea in the Arctic find incomprehensible the double standards exercised by many who live in gentler climes.

The fox populations increased and decreased in cycles, as did the price in southern markets. With a decrease in the demand for furs, people were forced to seek other employment. As the years went by, other occupations became available, some in the expanding government service, others in the mining and exploration industry. But, from the fifties until the building of the Distant Early Warning Line (radar stations every 50 miles across the Arctic coast, from Alaska to Greenland — a defensive line against Soviet military threat during the Cold War), a man's sole means of support came from his ability to hunt. If his family wanted to enjoy the comforts of life offered by the trading posts, he had also to trap to produce for the trader the skins and fur so highly prized in southern and European markets.

Living in the North and working with the people gives one a different perspective on the fur issues now so vociferously debated in the "developed nations" of the world. From the thirties to the sixties, the fur trade indeed introduced a real economy to the North. Good trappers who prepared their skins well and traded well were at the top of the local "economy". They had goods and were considered "rich". They were proud providers, looking after their families well.

When the fur market (on a world scale) crashed, these men found their skills worthless, and were unable to provide as much for their families, which by that time were used to the technologically advanced trade goods. This eroded their self-esteem and gave birth to the downward spiral of inadequacy and depression. The rise of the animal rights movement further depressed fur prices, and essentially put an effective end to the industry for most northerners. This was devastating to people who had always understood that trapping was an honourable and independent way of life.

Some former trappers have been able to make a transition to other work; but others, closely tied psychologically to the land, have not. The results have included chronic depression, abuse of alcohol, family violence, and, in some cases, even suicide. This is one of the serious problems that now faces the governments of all Canada's northern territories, and all agencies or organizations that work to improve living conditions for the people.

Chapter 18

In Journeys Oft...

Travelling on the land in the Arctic required a good deal of work and preparation. The dogs (*kinmit*) could only pull so much weight. This depended on the quality of the snow on the trail, the temperature, and the weather. The harsh cold meant that anything that could not be frozen required protection. Dog food had to be carried if its supply along the way was not assured. Personal gear was bulky and occupied a lot of space on the adliak.

For years, Harold Webster had been the community dentist in Coppermine. I inherited this duty with some trepidation. He initiated me into the practice (lacking formal training, I hesitate to apply the word "profession" here!), and I carried on after he left. On the

ABOVE: Numagina at Minto Inlet, prepared for the dazzling spring reflections from the snow. Photo: Canon Harold Webster.

sled, the first aid, medical, and dental supplies warranted a box of their own. Vials of Novocain and anaesthetics could be frozen, but had to be partially emptied to prevent breaking due to expansion by freezing. All medical supplies had to be kept scrupulously clean.

Garments and vessels for the delivery of the Sacraments were also carried on our sled. These were very primitive, because "Church" in a snowhouse hardly allows for ecclesiastical splendour.

Between camps, our food consisted of pre-frozen caribou steaks, frozen pre-sliced bread, and various kinds of dried peas, beans, etc. to make that all-important stew at night. Hardtack or pilot biscuits provided a bite for "mug-ups" (tea breaks on the trail).

Our sleeping gear (skins for bedding and sleeping bags), rifles, ammunition, a change of clothing, and the invaluable snowknife.... all had a place on the sled. Personal toiletries were modest - a toothbrush and some toothpaste, and a piece of soap - the latter only infrequently used on a trip.

Finally, the primus stoves and cans of kerosene for fuel had to be fitted in. Dogfood, which was bags of dried fish and seal blubber sufficient to get us to the first camp, were added essentials.

On long trips, we used eleven dogs, with a trained leader. The leader is the only one required to hearken and obey directional signals; the others just pull. "Gee" meant to turn right; "haw," meant left, and "whoa", to stop, a term that seemingly works for harnessed working animals anywhere.

The dogteam hitch used in the fifties in the Central Arctic had its source in Alaska, and is referred to as the "Nome hitch". In this hitch, the dogs are hitched to a central "gangline" in pairs, with a single leader. In the Eastern Arctic, the "fan hitch" is used. In this hitch, each dog is attached directly to a short line to the front of the sled.

For years, the comparative advantages of one hitch over another have been argued incessantly. In actual fact, as early photographs from the Canadian Arctic Expedition show, the "fan" hitch was prevalent in the Central Arctic before the "trapping for trade" era. With only two or three dogs per family, it was the woman who was harnessed as the leader, while the man, also in a simple harness, hauled away at the front of the sled.

During one of our journeys, I listened, fascinated, as Alfred Okkaituk described the calls the people used to encourage their dogs when he was a small boy. During their sled travel, the woman pulled with the dogs, in harness, so to speak. Consequently, any commands to the "leader" were unnecessary as the woman knew where they were heading. However, the man, also in harness, closer to the sled, uttered a repeated cry for further effort. As close as I can recall from Alfred's imitation, this was a sort of "Hurrrh!" He was not sure whether it was meant for the woman, or the dogs, and was unsure of its effectiveness.

After European goods became available, the need for dogs changed dramatically. This was affected by the change from the historic nomadic lifestyle of constantly being "on the move". A family with only their traditional belongings, clothing, tools, and hunting implements could move at will. However, the presence of large stone meat caches all over the Arctic provides evidence of the need to store dried meat, seal blubber, and seasonal hunting weapons.

But, with the move to a trapping economy came the necessity of operating traplines that often exceeded a hundred miles in length. Trade in fur led to the acquisition of a wide variety of trade goods, rifles, handloaders, ammunition, files, kettles, tarps, dog chains, etc. All combined to lead to a less uncertain way of life, and also resulted in a need for larger teams. There was simply more to carry.

The hunter and his family once wandered the inland hills stalking small herds of caribou. Women and children herded the caribou along rows of small stone *inuksuit* (locally called *inukhuit*), attempting to drive them to the men, armed with bows and arrows, and crouched behind stone blinds (*talus*). By the time we came to live in the Arctic, the hunters were able to procure their prey with rifles at a great distance. On the spring sea ice, they were able to obtain a harvest of basking seals that would feed their dogs for months. The rifle made it all so much easier.

With more meat, a good hunter could feed more dogs. It takes about as much food to feed a dog that is working hard as it does to feed a person. Conversely, in times of poor hunting, due to having more dogs, a hunter found himself having to acquire more game, and sometimes having to suffer if it was not available.

During the 1930s, dogteams steadily increased in size from two or three dogs to eight to ten dogs. The people who lived inland at Contwoyto Lake brought large quantities of fall caribou skins to the coastal posts for trade. These skins were shipped east to the Boothia Peninsula posts, where they were traded to the local people in that area. By the late 1950s, a successful hunter-trapper might own a team of sixteen dogs. Usually, eleven were used, pulling sleds up to 18 ft. (5.5 m) in length.

Teams of freighting dogs do not dash over the snow as is depicted in many films. A speed of 4 miles per hour (11 km/hr) is more likely, but can be maintained for hours at a time. The dogs walk, leaning into their harnesses and pulling mightily. A typical load might average 120 lbs (55 kg) per dog.

The sled itself requires a lot of attention. Its two runners are of sturdy wooden planks, which were, in our day, shipped in from the south at great expense. Long ago the people depended on drift-wood, tree logs which were carried down to the coast by mainland rivers and distributed all over the Arctic by sea currents. In our day, the planks came by ship.

In the spring, we could use steel runners. However, in the intense cold of winter, these were too abrasive, and we used the time-test-ed methods of the Inuit - a thin film of ice on a frozen running base of peaty mud. This required considerable advance planning and preparation.

In summer, we collected a quantity of loose earth, and carefully saved it for winter. After freeze-up, we melted a pot of frozen earth, making a firm paste, which, in turn we plastered on the wooden runners. When this layer was two to three inches deep, it was allowed to freeze, and then planed smooth.

Finally, a veneer of ice finished the job - warm water was spilled on a polar bear skin pad and run along the earthen base to develop a smooth surface, or sprayed from the mouth onto the runner and then polished with the bearskin mitt. The resulting icy surface glid-ed freely over the snow and sea ice, but was somewhat delicate, due to its inflexibility.

On any given day, this re-icing might need to be done three times or more.

We added a refinement to the mudding treatment. Should a part of the mud break away, we carried a bag of porridge oats, which could be cooked up to make a speedy and efficient repair.

Leaving camp in the morning was quite a problem, especially in the dark of the winter months. After being fed the previous evening, each dog required its "constitutional", for which travel was not interrupted to allow for any private convenience. As each dog deposited its droppings in mid- stride, great efforts were required to guide the sled away from the results, otherwise the ice coating would be lost before you were well on your way!

The sled dogs used by the Inuit in the 1950s were mostly of the breed now known as the Canadian Eskimo Dog. These are the abo-riginal dogs that came across the Bering Land Bridge with the Inuit. They are incredibly hardy, stocky, and have upstanding pricked ears and a double coat with thick underfur and stiffer guard hairs that shed the snow. These dogs can be almost any colour, grey, red, black, white with spots, or white with darker heads. Inuit dogs are champion eaters, and most undiscriminating in their tastes. They will eat almost anything of animal origin, including skin clothing, their harnesses, and sleeping skins. They had to be kept tied up, away from the travelling gear.

Undoubtedly some admixture of wolf genes have contributed to the breed somewhere in its development, although (fiction notwithstanding) no one really believes that interbreeding with wolves creates a better working animal. In our time there were many speculations about how to produce the perfect animal with a combination of the speed of the wolf and the strength of the husky. There were certainly some cross mating of the two, but these seldom resulted in better dogs.

Dogs have differing personalities. It is interesting how some can be very friendly to others and can be hitched up in partnership without any problems. Others develop antipathies and trouble results, especially at night when the long chain is set out and the animals tethered side by side in a long line. Some fights are unavoidable. In a newsletter I sent out in 1952, I included a mention of the loss of one of our faithful dogs:

"Once the dogs fight, unless restrained, they fight to the bitter end. Such an end was the sad lot of 'Mustang', one of our sled dogs. Two other dogs fought him one night in camp. Allonak and I, being very tired, slept through the fight, and did not hear a sound. The next morning, there lay Mustang, all covered in blood, obviously having had a bad time. We hoped he would survive, but he was far too weak. I had the unpleasant task of taking him away from camp onto the frozen sea and shooting him. It was the hardest thing I had to do during the whole trip."

Good dog drivers continually offer some encouraging words to the dogs, mainly to spur them on a little. Two favourite utterances, should the team slacken off a bit, were "Iglugaluit!" - "Lots of iglus ahead!" or "Tuktugaluit!" - "Lots of caribou!" Both were invariably untruths, and generally resulted in a very temporary effort to pull ahead with more effort. When one did actually come across either iglus or caribou, the dogs needed no urging at all. However tired they were, they took off at full speed!

Sometimes, one's leader may be either poorly trained or disobedient. On such occasions, constant shouting is necessary to get the team to behave. When travellers arrive after having travelled some distance, there is usually a man or two with a voice reduced to a hoarse whisper. It is unnecessary to enquire the reason for his laryngitis!

In the 1950s, before the coming of the snowmobile to the Arctic coast, a dogteam was vital to the survival of a family. The dogs were very well cared for, but were not considered pets, though young puppies were let into the iglu, and were the playtoys of the children.

Nursing bitches, if possible, were not used to pull. However, if it was necessary, they sometimes were decked out in interesting gear to protect their tender bellies, hairless because they were lactating. A piece of caribou calf skin was made into a little vest, and tied around the mother dog's middle, protecting her underside and teats from snow kicked up by her feet. The puppies were carried on the sled, usually in a box lined with caribou skin.

There was a real bond between dogs and owners. We regarded ours, especially a small bitch named "Trixie", with real affection. As in every relationship, there are times of some frustration, but, on the whole, we got along well. We discovered that problems might occur when affectionate indulgence went too far. One year, we had three pups which became special friends and pets to our children. They were familiar with all of us, but, as they grew up, I expected they would "pull their weight" with the others on the trail.

"Rob" was the most promising, and it crossed my mind that he might make a good leader. I took him on the long six week trip north, starting him in tandem with our veteran leader. (This is the usual way to train a potential leader as it has to follow the experienced animal, and thus, one hopes, learns the commands.)

Everything went well and, after some days, I decided to test Rob by placing him alone in the leader's position. All was set, the team harnessed and ready, and I stood proudly by the sled. I pulled the sled anchor out and called to the dogs, for "take off".

Rob took one stride, looked back, and led the whole team in a wide circle back to me! He approached me with obvious delight and leaped up to lick my face, to the vast amusement of my travelling companions. This ended his career as a leader. We found it difficult to make family pets into working dogs with any success.

Chapter 19

And More on Dogs...

Few ways of travel are more affected by weather than are dogteam journeys in the Arctic.

The word "blizzard" is only about a hundred years old. Various theories explain its origin — thought to be some sort of combination of "blow", "blast", and "bluster". In the North, the only word used for our "blizzards" was "blow", and blasting was as good a description as any. The local name was *pektuk*.

Our snowstorms differ mightily from those in the south, and our snow is far more likely to be minute ice crystals than soft fluffy stuff. When the wind rises in a "blow", it whips up fine particles of snow and blasts them with such power that the visibility drops to zero in

ABOVE: Anglican mission team working in rough ice. Photo: Canon Harold Webster.

a matter of minutes.

Each storm creates a special test of endurance with varying dis-comforts. Mostly one stays in camp during a "blow", as travel is emphatically unwise and life-threatening. Occasionally, however, a storm occurs unexpectedly, catching travellers unawares. In the increasing haze of blowing snow, the dogs vanish pair by pair until only the wheel dogs (closest to the sled) are visible.

The wind drives the fine snow into every nook and cranny. Your face becomes rimed with ice; even your eyelids freeze together. The only way to thaw the exposed face is with pressure from your bare hand. This sucks the heat from your hand, which then must be returned to the fur mitt to recuperate. The whole procedure must be repeated over and over. Despite our differing exposure prob-lems, travel in a bad storm is a miserable experience for men and dogs alike.

Travel in a blizzard is usually impossible, and the wise traveller stops and makes camp as soon as it is evident that a storm is approaching. However, if the families you are seeking are encamped upwind, it is possible to let the dogs follow their noses, and they will take you right to your destination.

If the wind is from the side, you are of course out of luck. Once, we were searching for a sealing camp, and the weather became so bad that we had to stop and camp. With the end of the storm and the coming of daylight, we could see the iglus not five hundred yards off to one side of our path.

All dogteams are fed at night after the day's travel is done. A full stomach hampers their motivation and pulling power, and can make them sick. As long as they are well fed, the husky dogs can work reliably in all kinds of weather.

Sickness occasionally sweeps through the Arctic, decimating the teams. One such sickness struck one year as I travelled with Alfred Okkaituk. Our dogs were always immunized for distemper and treated for worms, but, whatever this was, they did not escape it.

We were returning from Holman and, having lost one dog on the way, started a long overland portage. Amidst the rocky highlands, our remaining dogs began to drop. In all, we lost six animals. This left only five, and those were sick too. The good news (and we cer-tainly needed some) was that it was springtime, the days were long, and the sun warmed the land. Alfred and I took turns at being the "leader" and, at a slow pace, coached our team to the Hudson's Bay post some eighty miles away.

After our arrival we took a few days to rest and purchase some replacement dogs, then continued home to Coppermine. We reflected among ourselves that, in the Lord's service, one is never immune from troubles, but can be blessed and supported nonetheless with improvisation, determination, hard work...and some good dogs!

In springtime, the sun melts the surface of the snow during the day, making it soft and wet. The chill of the night refreezes it and this creates a crust on the surface that will support an animal like a fox, but not a dog. Dogs are supported by the crust for an instant, before it can break through with the edges of the icy crust causing injuries. Their feet quickly become cut and bleeding. To continue travel, you must have boots for the dogs. These are made from sealskin or canvas. Properly fitted and tied on each foot, boots protect the dog's feet from further damage and permit them to keep on working.

Travel on the land can be reasonably predictable in winter. However, travel on the sea ice is never predictable. After the short season of open water, the cold causes the salt water to freeze. If there is no wind while freeze-up occurs, the surface is quite smooth. However, if the wind is blowing, together with the strong influence of ocean currents, the sea ice can freeze into a scene rather like a bombed city. An excerpt from my journal:

"The string of islands we had been following soon disappeared, leaving a vast expanse of ice that stretched away to the distant shore of Victoria Island. This time, instead of the smooth and level sea ice to which we had become accustomed, a huge field of jagged ice pans in grotesque forms and shapes confronted us. It was euphemistic to call this 'rough ice'. It was more accurately described as a frozen catastrophe.

"We could not go around it or over it, and obviously could not go under it, we had to make our tortured way through it. I cannot adequately describe the process except to say that this was a prolonged experience of physical exertion for men and dogs."

Travel through rough ice (*maniilak*) is a science. One slip in guiding a laden sled through this "jungle" of ice could result in a crushed leg or irreparable damage to the sled itself. The process requires an understanding of physics, but it also requires brute strength. Pushing, heaving, gasping, shouting, stopping and starting, clambering over pressure ridges, chopping our way through jagged ice with an axe, freeing dogs entangled in the traces.... then having to do it all over again. One wonders whether there is an end to the challenge.

Personal discomfort increases as you struggle. Perspiration flows in rivulets under your fur clothing, which soon becomes a clammy burden, chilling you the instant you stop your exertions. Your muscles burn with fatigue, and the task seems endless.

On top of the battle to conquer the ice, there is the battle with the dogs. They work hard, and gulp snow at every opportunity. However they, especially the males, also have a compulsion to salute every little protuberance of ice. This leaves a trail of yellow "visiting cards", and infuriates the dog drivers. My companion and I did not always appreciate the uncountable times they paused in their work to fulfill their personal agendas!

Chapter 20

And Arriving...

Over the years, I undertook extensive journeys with some excellent and seasoned travellers, many of whom became good and close friends. Initially, there were Peter Kamingoak and Jack Allonak, both of whom served as my interpreters. They understood and spoke English (*Kavlunaktun*, meaning "like a white man") very well. Later, Alfred Okkaituk, Alec Algiak, and a veteran catechist from Holman, Sam Oliktoak, took over as my guides. They spoke only Inuinaktun, so all communications, on the trail and in the camps, were in the language of the people, in which I was gradually gaining some proficiency.

Our camps on the trail could be made either by building a small

ABOVE: Melting ice and cooking over the seal oil kudlik (lamp) in a snowhouse.
Photo: Canon Harold Webster

overnight snowhouse or by erecting a tent. Building a snow house required locating just the right type of snow, whereas a tent can be speedily set up and secured. We always carried a tent, especially in the springtime, when snowhouse building was less possible.

We developed a practical routine for setting up camp. Once the tent was set up, my companion unharnessed and fed the dogs, while I made the interior of the tent comfortable with the sleeping skins, and prepared our supper, melting chunks of ice over the primus stove. We ate together in the comfort of a nice warm tent, told and listened to stories, shared evening prayers, thanking the Lord for his care throughout the day, and drifted off to sleep. If Alec was with me, the evening included a couple of games of chess, which he dearly loved.

Once the primus stove was out, the big difference between a tent and an iglu became immediately apparent. The snow blocks of an iglu provided insulation, and the temperature was comparatively cozy all night, hovering around the freezing point. In a tent, the temperature inside quickly became the same as that outside the tent.

When tenting, we huddled in our sleeping bags fairly well clothed and, always very tired, slept the night away, the very hot tent of our suppertime only a memory. Of course, after a night's sleep in the freezing temperatures of an unheated tent (we could never carry enough fuel to use the primus stove except for cooking) our exhaled breaths created a frozen rim of ice around the openings of our sleeping bags. Upon awakening, we had to break through this rim, certainly a cooling "good morning" to the new day!

If we were travelling in a group, with other teams accompanying, we usually built a snowhouse to shelter all of us, far preferable to the nighttime chill of a tent. This allowed for a much better rest. If the weather turned bad, we simply extended our stay, sleeping away the storm.

In good weather, under the stars, with well-fed dogs curled snugly in the snow, and good companionship within the iglu, all seemed so peaceful.

Once in the hunting camps of the people, however, days and nights were filled with bustling activity. It was exhilarating, but sometimes overwhelming.

Arrivals were always exciting, heralded by much howling and excited barking of the resident dogs and of the arriving teams, joyful greetings, smiles, and general happiness. The people in these remote camps generally saw only two sets of visitors during the winter — the mission party, and the Royal Canadian Mounted

Police patrol. The RCMP patrol was invariably made up of understanding and friendly men, who annually visited all the camps to conduct censuses, issue hunting licenses, and record wildlife harvest figures.

Without radio communication, the people had only a rough idea when we would arrive. Their dogs knew first, and a general howl greeted us and roused the residents, who tumbled out of their snow houses with delight. The place for our dogs would be pointed out, and our gear unloaded by many helping hands. I was always ushered speedily to the host snowhouse, usually where the camp leader lived. Here, we were greeted with the first of many cups of tea!

In the most northerly regions of our parish, along the western coast of Victoria Island, every family lived in snowhouses. Usually there were only three families permanently residing at the Holman Island trading post, two of which lived in modest wooden shacks. But over the entire area, people were quite scattered, in camps that were usually three to four days travel apart. What they lacked in numbers, however, they made up in the warmth of their welcome to travellers. We were always mindful of the Scriptural imperative that the Gospel was to be preached to the "very ends of the earth", and that our Lord often had time for individuals and a very small group of people. While in a hunting camp, we were always invited to share the snowhouses of the residents; we never had to make our own.

A snowhouse is built by cutting down into hard-packed snow, and removing rectangular blocks about 3 ft. by 2 ft. by 8 to 12 inches (1 x .6 x .3 m) thick. These are shaped to create a spiral that curves up and in, creating a dome-shaped dwelling that is sealed by one key block set in the apex of the dome. Windows of clear ice admit light, and a small hole in the top allows warm air to escape. Due to the insulating qualities of the snow, a new snowhouse can be heated with a single candle. The entrance takes you into a narrow standing area from which blocks were removed, and which acts as a cold trap, allowing the warm air to remain inside the dome.

A snowhouse does not function well all winter. Body heat and the moisture from the breaths of the residents, along with the heat from the oil lamps, cause a layer of ice to form on the inside of the dome. Smoke from the lamps blackens parts of the inside as well. Eventually, the snowhouse loses its ability to insulate and becomes a frigid "ice-house". Even with careful ventilation and skillful trimming of the lamps, the once pristine appearance of the home of snow gradually deteriorates. This condition is accepted, and a well-built snow village is rarely abandoned unless local poor hunting demands a major move to another location.

On both sides of the entrance passageway, two sets of narrow snow walls are built to support lengths of wood on which are placed the stone seal oil lamp (known as a kudlik). A large family may have more than one of these elegantly simple lamps, which were the sole source of heat, light, and cooking power in the snowhouses of the past. The eldest daughter of the house, who is gaining experience at trimming the wick and maintaining this most important piece of household furnishings, tends the smaller lamp.

Above the lamps, wooden poles stuck into the walls of the iglu support oval drying racks of bent willow branches with a lacing of leather thongs. These poles also form a bar from which hang hooks for kettles and cooking pots. In the past, these pots were also made of soapstone, but, by the 1950s, these were of metal. The ice window above the entrance allows what exterior light there is to penetrate. The winter is long and dark at these latitudes far above the Arctic Circle, and most of the time the flickering candle-like flame of the kudlik is the one constant source of a gentle light.

A family iglu can be as much as eleven feet across. Half of it is taken up by a flat platform of snow, covered with caribou skins for sleeping. These skins are usually folded back until bedtime, and one's gear and sleeping bags pushed to the rear. People sit on the snow platform to eat and visit, and children play around (and sometimes on) the adults.

Usually a guest is given a sleeping place at the edge of the platform. Since I was tall, I always seemed to be placed in the middle, with various family members on either side. Within my own sleeping bag, I had privacy, but the sonorous snores of my well-filled bedmates echoed around the domed roof, sometimes enough as they say, "to wake the dead". However, weariness usually prevailed, and ushered me soon into a deep sleep.

In the days before matches were commonly available, one *kudlik* was burned all night with a low flame. Keeping it alight was the responsibility of the woman of the house. She seldom slept deeply, but dozed near the flame, awakening to adjust its height with a willow tending stick.

Upon awakening, most of us began the day with tea and raw frozen fish before dressing. The woman of the house would have arisen much earlier than the rest of us, and would ignite the full wick of the kudlik to boil the tea. Her daughter would follow suit with the smaller lamp.

Church in a snowhouse is memorable. The entire tiny community takes part, squeezing onto the platform to pray, sing hymns, and listen to the Scriptures and the teachings. I performed baptisms, marriages, and, of course, the sacrament of Holy Communion.

Sometimes the body heat of many people pushes the temperature in an iglu far above freezing, and the snow blocks forming the ceiling begin to melt and drip. I would be standing for the service of Holy Communion, and was the most suited to deal with the annoying drips. A snow block and snowknife stood by the entrance, and it was an easy matter to bend down, cut a small block of snow, and press it to the dripping spot on the ceiling, where it absorbed the moisture immediately, stopping the drips.

I recall one occasion in a snowhouse on Victoria Island. My hosts had built a small alcove in the side of the iglu for a bitch and her pups, close to the board holding the kudlik. I set up the Cup and the Paten for the service on this board. As I conducted the service, the pups suckled noisily. Now and again, one little creature would lose its place and squeal a complaint. It didn't spoil the flow of the service to reattach the little thing, and on we would go. I thought of another similar scene long ago, when the Lord of all creation came into our world in the company of the beasts of the field and amongst his people in equally humble circumstances.

Chapter 21

All in the Family...

The years of the 1950s in the Arctic were a veritable window into the past, allowing us to learn what life must have been like generations before.

The availability of some of our southern technology through fur trading had greatly reduced the hardship and suffering of former times. However, the ancient spirit of interdependence and sharing was still quite strong. Even in the larger camps, no woman would make tea, set out the frozen fish or cook fish heads, seal, caribou, or polar bear meat without popping her head out of the snowhouse porch or tent flap, and announcing the main course, usually the only course. If it were polar bear, then the cry would be

ABOVE: A puppy joins a sleeping child on the Unipkak family sled.

"Nanuktugitti!" ("Come and eat bear meat!") "Teatugitti!" ("Come and have tea!") was a common call, but gallons of tea seemed to be a part of every meal.

Seal hunting was the main occupation in the northern part of our parish in winter. In earlier times, there were very special relationships involving the dividing up of a ringed seal, the smaller of the two most common seal species in the area. The successful hunter shared certain parts of the animal with special hunting partners. For instance, a man might honour a close friend by having him share the seal flippers, a special delicacy. These two might then be referred to as *upatitkatik* ("sharers of the flippers").

Other parts of the seal were shared with everyone, as far as they would go. If a hunter managed to harpoon the much larger bearded seal, he called for help in landing it. Once it was safely on the ice, there is a "free-for-all" in which everyone speedily slices up whatever he can get. The veteran missionary, Herbert Girling, wrote of often having to deal with cut hands and wrists after a bearded seal dismembering competition. Those customs have long gone now.

In another camp where I was staying in the snowhouse of an older couple, the hunter brought home the only seal anyone caught that day. His wife immediately skinned it inside the house. As she began to cut off the blubber, youngsters from neighboring iglus poked their heads in the door, holding bowls. The old lady proudly apportioned out to each a slice of blubber for the lamps. Everyone would be eating a share of the meat later.

When we arrived at a camp, we usually were required to spend a long time answering questions as to how things have been with everyone we had visited on our travels, most of whom our hosts knew, or had heard about. We recited births and deaths, discussed food supplies, fur abundance or lack thereof, and told stories about any adventure that might be of interest or a source of hilarity. All these stories were interspersed with calls for further eating, of course.

Then there were amusements. A rope can be strung through the iglu, poked through the walls and held with toggles on the outside. The youths and children put on an acrobatic display while the rest of us would lean back and show our admiration. Other games, such as *nuglugak* (a spearing game), or string games may follow. These are similar to the familiar children's "cat's cradle" games, with a northern flair, in which the figures have northern names - "man carrying a kayak", "two caribou", "rocks falling"... Gambling games were not uncommon, but were not taken seriously, as they were not gambling for money in those times.

The decade of the 1950s represented the last years when all the people, from the eldest to the youngest, could communicate in a common language. All lived under one roof, and people of all ages related to each other. There was no TV, no Nintendo, and the intense desire for mechanized speed had not yet reached this far coast. Knowledge was passed on verbally, through story and song, from elders to the youth. Many quiet evenings were spent in the half-light of the snowhouse, listening to tales of the past, to legends and lore. Many elders today look back on this time with intense nostalgia, whilst knowing it could not last.

There are so many distractions challenging our northern youth today, including too much TV, alcohol, drugs, concentration on speedy snow machines, gambling, and a lack of understanding of their place and value in society. All these were unheard of in the 1950s. From childhood, boys were trained to be as their fathers were, hunter-providers and trappers. They knew what skills they had to develop, and could be proud when they mastered them. The girls knew they would be mothers, seamstresses, and tenders of the seal oil lamps, and likewise were proud to do these things well. Both men and women had their functions and roles, and for the most part, fulfilled them. Not all families and communities were without problems; but, looking back over the years and the changes, these problems seemed very manageable compared with what lay ahead.

Iglu life in those days involved a great deal of work, especially for the women, whose lives revolved around the needle and thread. Adult women were skilled seamstresses. They knew how to make, just by using a certain type of stitching, sealskin boots (*kamiks*) that were totally waterproof. When I was fitted for my winter fur clothing, the lady chosen for the task measured me quickly and proficiently, without the benefit of any tape measure at all. I later discovered that the ladies do this by comparing the subject's size with that of her husband, and designing the clothing appropriately. Whatever the technique, it resulted in perfectly fitting clothing for me, every time.

The use of needle and thread by the women carried beyond clothing. In the fifties, most women of forty years or more were elaborately tattooed on their faces, hands, and arms. This seemed to be done solely as a custom of fashion. The process was extremely painful. A bone or copper needle, threaded with soot-blackened sinew, was drawn under the skin, in and out to create solid or dotted lines. I recall discussing this with a younger lady one time. She had only a couple lines on her fingers. I asked why she did not have more, and she replied, "When my mother did it, I screamed so much that she took pity on me and stopped."

Many of the older women seemed to have their teeth worn down to mere stubs. This resulted from years of working and softening skins. The skins used in the Arctic are not tanned; they are allowed to dry, then softened by scraping and working the fibres with special dull scrapers of metal or stone. The edges must be further softened to allow sewing, so the women chewed them. The soles of waterproof sealskin *kamiks* in our area were crimped into a boatlike shape, each fold placed precisely by biting and drawing the skin through the teeth.

Clothing maintenance required a lot of work as well. Boots of caribou and seal alike become stiff from wear, dampness, and perspiration. They are worked and chewed to make them soft again. It is the lady of the house that accepts this task, as she does so many others. And she performs these services for her guests as well. My boots were always included in the group being worked on by the women in the group we visited.

Life for Inuit women was difficult in more than just the daily work. Their very lives were at risk at birth, in the old days.

Arranged marriages, and births under primitive conditions were normal for the people of the Arctic coast. Enormous pressures for survival also fostered other customs. One was the exposing of female infants at birth, allowing them to die immediately. Male hunters were so necessary to these small groups of nomadic peoples that female babies could at times not be allowed to tie up their mother's reproductive cycle. She needed immediately to become pregnant again, to produce, in answer to a commonly shared hope, a son. None of this was discussed or planned; it just happened. We know today that this practice was not unique to the Arctic.

In the local culture, a child was not considered to be a human being until a name was given; the name endowed personhood. Consequently, exposing female infants at birth had in no way any stigma of infanticide.

The practice of not allowing female infants to live resulted in an imbalance of the sexes - too many men. Additionally, should a good hunter demonstrate his prowess by taking more than one wife, other men were deprived. As a result, polyandry (one woman having more than one husband) was sometime practiced. This sometimes led to jealousies and violence.

Ikey Bolt told me about Ulukhak, an excellent hunter who had two wives and then stole a third. The robbed husband watched from his tent, shot Ulukhak through the thigh, and then walked to him as he lay on the ground. The wounded man asked to be finished off, the husband complied, and that was the end of the business. The killer took his own wife back again.

The people are not at all embarrassed to discuss the violence of former times. I remember sitting with one group whose conversations were entirely about relatives who had been involved in murders in years past. Everyone in the group could name such a relative.

Times were changing, however. Algiak told me that his father killed another man but, thereafter, never forgot the incident, and told his son always to avoid killing human beings.

A greater respect for the intrinsic value of human life was an expanding influence of the teaching of the Gospel in this culture.

In addition to spiritual services, we provided medical services. Our medical box was a vital part of our travelling supplies. In the days before the trading posts stocked sweetmeats, candies, and soft drinks, and before sugar became a necessary part of every cup of tea, the teeth of the people were in excellent shape. However, occasionally someone had a toothache, and my services were required. I was generous in the use of the local anesthetic, and gained something of a reputation as a tooth-puller. This may not have been deserved; my patients' gums were so thoroughly deadened that they felt little or no pain.

I was less knowledgeable with more serious illnesses or injuries. Whatever can be said for isolation and its blessings, the lack of easily available medical care certainly made things more difficult than they are today. The best we could do was to recommend that the sick person be taken to the nearest trading post where a physician could advise treatment by radio.

For my ministry (and myself), the most valuable aspect of those days was in getting to know the people by travelling with them, by staying in their homes, by sharing good times and bad. I learned from them, and I am sure they learned all my weaknesses as, initially, they had to put up with my obvious ignorance about their way of life.

It was also a gift, though not always appreciated at the time, to be exposed to the use of the language by the "immersion" method. This later led me to an important translating challenge, one that was to have a profound impact on my ministry. The people of the Central Arctic were in great need of translations if the word of God and the liturgy were ever going to be expressed in their own dialect.

Chapter 22

Nunamiut - People of the Land

In their early history, the Copper Inuinait spent their summers hunting caribou and musk oxen inland far from the sea. However they never strayed too far south, into what could be considered Dene ("Indian") territory, as the Dene tribes considered the Inuinait their enemies.

As trading opportunities increased with the establishment of the trading posts, better relationships developed with their neighbors to the south. A pioneer trader, D'arcy Arden, established a trading post at Great Bear Lake, and Inuit from the coast began travelling inland to trade, especially after being encouraged to do so by the members of the Canadian Arctic Expedition (1913-1918).

ABOVE: Well-dressed man on the trail. Photo: Canon Harold Webster

By the 1930s, the demand for fox fur and caribou skins encouraged a number of families to spend their entire year inland, including many who traded at the posts at Coppermine and Bathurst Inlet. Once these people had established the habit of living inland, they made only two trips to the coast. Mainly the men made the trip at Christmas, but entire families made the second trip, at Eastertime.

Caribou populations across the Arctic experienced a low point in their cycles during the 1950s. The lack of caribou caused a severe lack of suitable skins for clothing throughout the Central Arctic. This created a market for good clothing skins. Sealskins are never a good substitute for the warmth that caribou skin can provide.

The trading posts at Bathurst Inlet and Coppermine bought as many skins as they could, shipping these skins to posts in the east, on the Boothia Peninsula and King William Island.

Good supplies of caribou skins depended upon the hunting camps being located in the right place to meet the migrating herds. This was by no means an exact science; the migratory routes were not always the same, though they were in the same general area. People travelling on foot did not have a good view of large areas of land. You could be in one valley or on one ridge, and miss thousands of caribou passing a single valley away. Slight changes in traditional migratory patterns could have devastating results for the Inuit hunters.

Our visits to the Inlanders occurred in the "dark days" of January, at the coldest time of year. We always travelled with the knowledge that there were no re-supply posts either coming or going, but with a confidence that provision could be found. Alec Algiak was my companion on each occasion. He had lived inland for many years previously, and knew the country well. Our lives depended on his skill in navigation and in hunting.

When we travelled in winter in the northern part of our area, on the sea ice, the scenery was usually unchanging, just snow and ice, with perhaps the glimpse of an arctic fox, and rarely, a polar bear. To the south, all life is above the ground, so we often saw wildlife - small herds of caribou, foxes, wolves and wolverines and their tracks, small flocks of ptarmigan, or the occasional raven, gyrfalcon or arctic hare.

Alec knew the land with a familiar intimacy, and would have made an admirable tourist guide. As we travelled, he kept up a lively commentary on points of special interest - places where his long-dead forebears had lived, hunted, and died, lakes and river-crossings where caribou could be hunted in summer from kayaks, and places where he had camped in the past. He told stories of all sorts. The time on the trail passed swiftly with the telling of these tales.

Travelling with the people exposed me to many stories and much local lore. An elder called Aluyak, highly skilled with a kayak, once told me that if you are paddling up to a swimming bull caribou in your kayak in order to spear it, watch how his antlers are positioned. If they are tilted with the outer branches and its ear close to the water, don't get too close, as he will surely sweep his antlers, over-turning your kayak.

The inland camps were very different from the snowhouse villages to the north. Utter dependence on the caribou was evident everywhere. These people often lived in caribou skin tents year round, banking the tents with snow in the winter. Their tents were made of the thickly furred winter skins, with windows made from the translucent lining of a caribou's stomach.

Soapstone lamps were smaller, fueled with the backfat of the caribou and used for cooking. In our time, small stoves made from 10-gallon gasoline drums with a stovepipe through the roof of the tent provided heat in the tents. These were fueled with wood. The treeline was not far to the west, so trips could be made there for wood.

All clothing was made of caribou skin, and was extremely well made and warm. We ate caribou meat in all forms - raw, cooked, dried, frozen. In addition to muscle meat, we ate the tongues, backfat, hearts, eyes, brains, and the very marrow of the bones, which was delicious in the intense cold. It was not unusual to see the head of a caribou, skinned and deantlered, looking out at you from a large cooking pot. People would pick off favourite bits, much as southerners select delicacies from the carcass of a roast turkey.

The caribou suffered from insect infestations in the summer. Mosquitoes and blackflies could drive a herd into a frenzy. Then there were the warble flies, which deposit their eggs on the hair of the caribou in the summer. These eggs quickly hatch and the larvae burrow through the skin and migrate through the animal, ending up under the skin of the back, where they bore small holes through which they breathe while continuing to feed on the blood, lymph, and muscle of the caribou. A freshly killed caribou may have almost a hundred of these high protein white bean-like grubs under the hide of its back. These were avidly collected and eaten, the sweet-meats or candies of the children in the times before the trading posts offered more attractive (but less healthful) alternatives.

The dogs also lived almost entirely on caribou. Though it was not as nutritious as seal meat, they seemed to do well on it.

The barrenground caribou in the mainland Central Arctic are members of a large herd called the Bathurst herd. They winter in the forest to the north and east of Great Slave Lake, sometimes near Yellowknife, and begin their northward migration in March. The cows travel almost to the coast, calving in early June in some of the most remote areas imaginable. Young bulls accompany them, but the older bulls do not walk all the way to the coast, preferring to wander in all-male herds in the central barrenlands near Contwoyto Lake, and along the upper Burnside, Hood, and Mara Rivers. They are joined by the returning cows and calves in August, and wander the inland barrenlands until the rut in October, by which time they are back at the treeline.

The Inlanders would meet the caribou on both migrations, but the fall migration was the most important to them; to miss the herd would cast grave doubt on their ability to survive the winter in the Barrenlands. Each family required about three hundred caribou to meet the needs of people and dogs for the winter. They did fish, but fish were regarded as more a supplement to their diet than a staple. They truly depended on the caribou.

Inlanders had opportunities for a big hunt that might provide them with food for months. Their coastal cousins, who seemed to have to struggle for food all year round, sometimes envied them. On the surface, it does seem as though a big hunt offers more security, but it also involves an enormous amount of work, which has to be done in a short period of time.

Before winter claimed the inland barrens, all the meat has to be preserved by drying or freezing, and put up in caches that can be located when the meat is needed. All skins have to be scraped and dried, and carefully stored; winter clothing has to be prepared, and supplies of fuel prepared. Hunts for wandering small herds continue throughout the winter.

It was a precarious life indeed. If the migratory herds chose another route, then disaster might strike, causing people to starve, or resulting in a forlorn cavalcade of survivors trying to make their way to the coast in the dead of winter, with no hope of food being cached along the way.

TOP: Children in porch of iglu at Nuvuk (Berkeley Point) opposite Banks Island in 1953. Drift timber from the Mackenzie River was often utilized by people in his area.

ABOVE: A freshly-made iglu provided good insulation from the elements, and could be lighted with a single candle. Temperature inside was kept at or slightly below the freezing point.

PREVIOUS PAGE: Games and stories helped to pass the time in the iglus of the past. Here Margaret Ikegyuak does gymnastics on a thong strung through the snowhouse

ABOVE: The Niakoaluk
family in an iglu at
Nauyat. In back, father
Harry Niakoaluk
reclines on the snow
bench. Front row,
left to right: Margaret
Ikegyoak, John
Alikamik, Joseph Alukik,
Flossie Papidluk
(sewing), Effie Akhak.

RIGHT: The custom of
tattooing seems to have
been done for fashion
purposes only. Here
Emma Noanikuk
threads a needle,
showing the tattoos
on her arms and face.

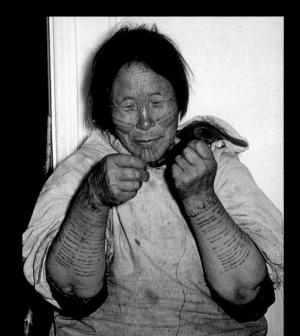

ABOVE: Boys usually
started caribou hunting
when barely 10 years
old. Here, Jimmy Kudlak
poses with caribou he
has shot at Naloayuk,
on Prince Albert Sound,
Victoria Island.

LEFT: Caribou were
skinned as soon as
possible, before
freezing. Ruth
Negiyunak is skinning.

RIGHT: Snow goggles
helped prevent painful
snow blindness while
travelling in the spring.
Sam Kuniluk wears
goggles of caribou
antler. His breath has
condensed around
his ruff.

ABOVE: High in protein and without any sugar, warble fly larvae were the sweetmeats of the Eskimo children of the past. Here Ida Aivik collects larvae from under the skin of a caribou's back.

LEFT: Hikhiks (arctic ground squirrels) were trapped for food and for their skins, which were used to make clothing for toddlers.

TOP: People at their camp at Ennadai
Lake during times of famine in 1958.
They had just been told they would be
picked up the next day by military aircraft,

ABOVE: People in qangmak at Ennadai
Lake during starvation times in 1958.

ABOVE: John and Angela Sperry outside the mission house in Coppermine, springtime 1963.

LEFT: Elizabeth MacLaren Sperry.

TOP: Modern travel – in a box pulled at great speed over the ice by snowmobile. Riding in one of these in the dark, under a tarpaulin, was rather like practicing for your own funeral!

BELOW: Snowmobiles come to the North! Hunting ptarmigan by snowmobile.

TOP: Tent hostel at Coppermine
(Kugluktuk).

ABOVE: Hostel students saying "grace"
before a meal.

TOP: Tent hostel at Coppermine, with
Helen Sperry at the right.

ABOVE: Betty Sperry teaching girl's group
at St. Andrew's Mission.

ABOVE: Comfort for
the elders in their own
language, Nellie Nalikak
and Sperry, in her home
in Kugluktuk.

LEFT: Child in black
fur ruff, Taloyoak.

TOP: Christening ceremony at Bathurst Inlet, 1995. Sperry, Karen Ongahak, Kevin Ongahak Kapolak, George Haniliak Kapolak, Jessie Hagiolak Kapolak.

ABOVE: Teaching others about the North and her people, Bathurst Inlet Lodge, 1999. Bishop Sperry with Caroline Olsen and Sarah Drummond, both from the US.

FOLLOWING PAGE: Joseph Alukik performing gymnastics on a thong in iglu at Nauyat near Holman.

Chapter 23

Starvation

In the past, starvation was a dreaded reality in the Arctic, especially for those people who lived inland. In the days before radios, aircraft, and government intervention, the people often felt the bite of hunger. Deaths due to starvation were not uncommon. All that was necessary was to be in the wrong place, and miss the caribou.

It is at times of life-threatening disaster that the influence of ancient taboos can place groups of people in mortal danger. In late April of 1957, I witnessed a vivid proof of this among the inland Caribou Inuit of the Keewatin (now called Kivalliq) Region to the west of Hudson Bay.

Bishop Donald Marsh had asked me to accompany him on trav-

ABOVE: Hungry times carve their marks in the faces of the elders. Bill Wikiak, near Coppermine (Kugluktuk).

els to the Eastern Arctic. This was my first visit to the part of the diocese that I would later be responsible for as the third Bishop of the Arctic. We flew from community to community in a single-engine aircraft, landing on skis. We met with the people, conducted services, and in general carried on our ministry by air instead of dogteam.

We finished our tour at Churchill, and parted, Bishop Marsh to return to his home in Toronto. Our pilot, Ken Stockall, was to fly me back to Yellowknife prior to my return home to Coppermine.

Before we took off, a government agent asked us to stop at a small weather station at a place called Ennadai Lake, about 250 miles inland from Arviat, then called Eskimo Point. Here, a group of inland people was in serious trouble from starvation. We were to let them know that the Royal Canadian Air Force would be flying in the next day, to evacuate them all and to move them to another camp where food was more readily available.

We agreed, and flew northwest, landing at the weather station on a Tuesday, April 30, 1957. We were met by about fifteen people — men, women, and children. All were obviously starving. They were living in the sooty shells of *iglus*, with tarpaulins draped over the disintegrating walls. They were gaunt and their clothing hung on their wasted frames. Their story was pathetic.

This group of people depended on the caribou for sustenance, but the caribou had not come. All caribou seemed to have vanished from the land, for reasons unknown to the people. The caribou just did not pass along their usual trails. The people had long since eaten all their dogs, and were trying to cook squares of caribou hide with the hair scraped off. We gave them what food we carried on our plane, but as our aircraft was completely inadequate for a rescue mission, their hope depended on the promised relief plane.

Our news, which I was able to communicate, despite a different dialect, was that a larger plane would come on the morrow to take them to a new hunting area. This news was met with great joy. No one protested about being moved - they were obviously relieved and grateful.

We visited the weather station, and asked the staff, "Why? Why are they starving?" The answer was that, while the people would accept a few bits of food from the station, they clearly depended on caribou. The lakes had plenty of fish, yet they would not fish.

For that group of Inlanders, fishing was taboo. According to their beliefs, if you fish, then the spirit powers of the caribou will not send the animals your way. So, no one would fish. I had never observed, among our own people on the Arctic coast, any camp under the grip of a taboo this strong. I had some doubts about the truth of such an explanation, and pursued it a bit. However, from what they said, it seemed true. Seeing that they were subsisting on boiled squares of old caribou hide instead of the succulent flesh of available lake trout was evidence too convincing to deny.

For the survivors in this little group, all ended safely. The government plane arrived, and the entire group was taken to the inland trading post of Padlei, an area that offered better hunting.

Today, there is an increasingly popular attitude in the North that, during the starvation years of the 1950s, Inuit were moved without any consultation and against their will. In this case, that certainly was not so; the Ennadai people were more than grateful for a government initiative which promised some security and deliverance from what might well have resulted in a miserable death. It is clear from their demeanor and words that the promise of a practical rescue was happily received, and that any notion of enforced "deportation" or "relocation" was ludicrous.

From my viewpoint, this inland tragedy was a clear example of the enormous influence and power of taboos in the lives of the Inuit of those times. As in the case at Ennadai Lake, even the threat of slow starvation would not allow a break in their determination to await the mercy of the land animal spirits.

Not all taboos were universally observed. About the same time the Ennadai people were in distress, another group, not far away, also had missed the caribou migration. However, in their case, fishing through the ice was not prohibited. They had a difficult time; some perished, but some also survived.

However, unhappily, the extreme privation in that tiny camp led to a double killing: a desperate woman struggling to reach another camp with her children, one of whom froze to death, and all the later drama of a well-publicized enquiry.

As tempting as it is to assign a mindset, philosophy, emotions, or reactions to any group of Inuit in times of extreme privation, doing so is risky. Information is not processed the same as in our culture; their own beliefs and traditions control thought and behaviour. This is especially relevant when an entrenched conviction can imperil the survival of an entire group through the fear of breaking a single taboo. Rather, it is the survivors themselves, after the crisis is over, who are able to offer clarification and convincing accounts, especially when they are able to reflect and describe the events in their own language, without the pressure of being interrogated by outsiders or guided in their responses.

Additionally, in present times, when it is fashionable to question and even protest the fact that Christianity did challenge some aspects of native spirituality, the witness of aboriginal people them-selves is singularly appropriate.

One year, I was to accompany an Inlander from our own parish, Alec Algiak, as a delegate to the Church's General Synod in Winnipeg. Alec was invited to address the assembly, and took the opportunity to express his profound gratitude for the mission of the Church in the North, and for the proclamation of the Gospel of Christ having been taken to his people. I interpreted for him as he told the story of the difference his personal experience as a Christian made to him in a critical situation.

Here is his story:

"We were inland in the late summer, and the caribou had not returned on their migration. There was hunger among us, and the children were crying. Every day, we men, with one dog each, walked out in different directions to spy out the land, looking for caribou.

"At last, at a place where I waited, I could see four caribou coming towards me.

"In those days, we Inlanders, after using all our store-bought ammunition, made our own bullets with lead. These were not always reliable. I had a homemade shell in my rifle, and fired it at the first caribou. I missed, and then could not eject the casing as it was stuck in the breech. I tried to loosen it with my penknife and my fingernail, but only broke both. It would not move, and the caribou were getting closer and closer.

"So, I knelt down and prayed that God would come to my aid. I thought of how needy we were and how the children cried with hunger. Then, I looked up, and remembered that inside the leather collar my dog wore there was a thin band of steel.

"I took my broken penknife and cut open the collar, took the band of steel and used it as a ramrod to dislodge the casing. Then I reloaded and killed all four caribou. I did not forget to thank the Lord for help-ing me to clear my mind."

You can imagine the impact this had on the Synod. This report came as a breath of fresh air to a group usually absorbed with a wide variety of dry reports and statistical analysis.

Alec's father, and certainly his grandfather, living without ever hearing that there was a supreme deity with a compassionate con-cern for His creation, and finding themselves in a similar situation, would naturally conclude that this was bad luck caused by a malig-nant spirit, an offence caused by a broken taboo, or even a curse from an enemy. They would have given up and accepted fate. Alec had an alternative.

There is a word commonly used among the Inuinait (and indeed among all Inuit): *aiyungnangman*. It means, essentially, "It can't be helped", and is frequently used when people feel that control of events is out of their hands. These words survived from a time when human beings were at the mercy of an unseen world of spirits, rendering them helpless.

In more recent times, *aiyungnangman* is used for all manner of situations even when the matter at hand could indeed be helped with a little more thought and attention. However, the use grew out of a genuinely depressing philosophy, fostered by a feeling of being dominated by external forces.

Alec Algiak and his contemporaries, who were acutely aware of the tenuous nature of life, were deeply grateful for the sharing of the Good News in Christ by the missionaries of the Church, and the freedom that these new beliefs provided. Despite their initial unfamiliarity with the concepts of Christianity, they considered it unthinkable to be demanding apologies for the bringing of a truth that exchanged fear and uncertainty for the liberating power of the Gospel.

There were other major changes occurring in the North, including changes in the way the government regarded the peoples of the Northlands and looked after their interests.

Not many years after the Ennadai Lake experience, our Inlanders from Coppermine missed the main fall caribou migration, and concluded they would have to trek to the coast, weakened by hunger. Without any means of communicating their plight, they began the slow journey in a weakened state, people with the strongest teams arriving first with the news. Immediately, rescue dog teams raced south to assist, and all the people were brought to Coppermine. For a year or two, the vast hinterland of the Central Barrenlands was devoid of people.

A number of families eventually returned to live at Contwoyto and Pellatt Lakes. They brought with them communications equipment with which they could summon help. These days, anyone who establishes an outpost camp away from a settlement is equipped with either a CB or high-frequency radio and can call for help at a moment's notice. An increasing number of people are now using satellite phones, which are extremely reliable.

But the term *aiyungnangman* is still used, mostly by people who have achieved less control of their lives, and who may wish to avoid responsibility for their actions.

In modern times, physical starvation no longer haunts the daily lives of Arctic dwellers, unless self-inflicted abuse invites it for oneself (or, sadly, for one's family). Settlement of the Inuvialuit and Inuit land claims and increased participation by aboriginal peoples in the governments of both the Northwest Territories and Nunavut has engendered sweeping changes, and ample opportunities for all, in terms of education, job opportunities, and personal development.

Indeed, it is a Christian belief that, to be truly human, a sense of integrity and fulfillment must include the whole person. The challenge to achieve a meaningful lifestyle of fulfillment and purpose is, of course, common to humanity in every part of the world. Central to the Gospel proclamation is the idea that spiritual rebirth be accompanied by growth in health, of body, mind and spirit. This applies to all, and certainly to northern peoples.

Chapter 24

A Partner of Promise

The year 1952 brought great changes in my life. After a period of training and familiarization with the people and life of the Church in the Arctic, I was more or less ready to take over full responsibility for the Coppermine parish, especially as Canon Webster and his family were leaving for a mission in the Mackenzie Delta.

My two years of Arctic service had also readied me for a new partnership in the mission - I was to be married! According to the rules of the Diocese, every newly ordained missionary was required to serve two years in order to learn something of the people, the culture, and the language before permission was granted for marriage.

Elizabeth MacLaren and I met in 1947 at Emmanuel College. She

ABOVE: Partners of promise, John R. Sperry and Elizabeth MacLaren Sperry at their wedding in Coppermine, 1952. Photo: Canon Harold Webster.

spent her early years in Northeast England, in South Shields, where she was born. Her father, having lost an eye in the battle of the Somme in World War I, moved the family down to Kent, where he was able to find appropriate employment. She continued her education at Belvedere.

At that time, prospective brides were required to complete a questionnaire regarding their Christian commitment, experience, and willingness to serve in a joint ministry. Furthermore, they had to accept all the hardships and privations of living in the Arctic. At the time of completing the questionnaire, they could only imagine what all of that might mean.

Betty was a fully committed Christian, and had already begun preparation for missionary service. When we met, she had already gained her Registered Nurse accreditation. Following our engagement, she completed a final year of midwifery training in London, before the Diocese accepted her.

In 1951, Betty sailed for Canada and an assignment at All Saints' Anglican Hospital in Aklavik, in the Mackenzie Delta. This was her decision, a necessary test to determine whether a call to the Arctic really was a vocation, divinely ordained for a lifetime of service in the North. She wanted to make sure it was not a short-term sojourn prior to a longed-for return to warmer and more agreeable climes. Betty is a strong person with firm scruples and was adamant about this; only after serving, alone, in the North, would she travel to Coppermine to be married.

Mission hospitals in the 1950s were places where service to the sick was performed under conditions unimagined in North America today. The Aklavik hospital was no exception. There were usually about a hundred patients. Of these some eighty were hospitalised due to tuberculosis. The night duty nurse was alone, calling for help only in emergencies. While local help was available during the days for strenuous duties, the night nurse was required to replenish the wood furnace with five-foot lengths of logs in order to maintain a consistent heat in the wards throughout the night watches. Betty's job was not an easy one, physically or mentally.

Now, looking back over half a century of Arctic service, Betty and I sometimes reflect on the high expectations of the Diocese in the early days, especially in terms of personal commitment to God's call. In many cases, accepted candidates offered long and fruitful service on this frontier of the Church's mission. Betty and I have never regretted our choices made so long ago.

When the news of my coming marriage was passed around Coppermine, the usual assumption was that we had been promised to each other as small children; that our parents had arranged the match. The practice of arranged marriages was then very strong along the Arctic coast (and would remain so for many years).

Adult couples that by choice were neighbours, friends, and hunting partners mutually knew the hunting and sewing abilities of each person. Consequently, new parents felt that they and their children would benefit by being linked in marriage to contemporaries most likely to be taught and brought up "correctly" with the skill and energy of their parents. They simply did not understand that Betty and I had made our own decisions in the matter of our marriage.

When we were married, apart from the few southern couples in the community, we were the only couple that had NOT been promised and predestined for each other as infants.

As it turned out, Betty travelled to Coppermine with Bishop Donald Marsh, who was making his annual episcopal visitation to the missions along the coast. Upon completing his visitation in Coppermine, he would accompany the Websters to their next assignment in Aklavik.

The Bishop had also brought with him a camera crew. As part of its historic missionary commitment, the Church had commissioned a film of its missions around the world, entitled *The Power Within*. In those days, the mission commitment included work on Indian reservations in the south, as well as service in Japan and India, and in the Arctic.

For the portion on Arctic missions, Jack Allonak and I were to be filmed driving dogs over the local river ice and snow, clad in full winter clothing, although it was springtime and quite warm. We were also to hold a "service" in a snowhouse with an Inuit family.

The snowhouse had been built, the family and I sat on the platform awaiting our "cues". I was seated close to the wall. The camera was ready, but the cameraman decided the aperture carved out of the side of the snowhouse to admit enough light for filming was not large enough. He had watched the iglu-builders wield the long snowknife with dexterity. So, borrowing a snowknife, he plunged it through the wall of the iglu with a flourish. The tip of the blade stopped, literally touching my left eyelid! Bystanders yanked the knife out of his hand and enlarged the hole with more skill, and the sequence was finally filmed. Instead of what could have been a tragic interruption, we completed our contribution to the film, and the wedding took place early the same evening, on Thursday, April 24, 1952.

Bishop Marsh conducted the service, mainly in English so that the newly arrived bride understood both what she and, indeed, the groom, were promising. Hymns and other parts were in Inuinaktun. Betty's white bridal dress and white-iced wedding cake were both carefully shepherded from Aklavik, and occasioned a great deal of interest, amusing in a world which presented an abundance of white for most of the year. Of course, after the service, there was a small reception in the Hudson's Bay Company house, followed by a community feast consisting of rice and raisins with buns, and gallons and gallons of tea. A spirit of rejoicing was evident everywhere.

All in all, it was a very special day.

In the years following, Betty more than fulfilled her promises made in the questionnaire. At first, before the lay leadership in our church became stronger, she conducted services when I was absent. She visited the sick, started Sunday school in our parish, and introduced the concept of women's meetings. She also served for some time as the community nurse.

Within a week of our wedding, her midwifery knowledge was put to the test. Jack Allonak's wife Martha went into labour, and Betty handled the birth. I was recruited to assist (not the usual assignment on one's honeymoon), and thereby witnessed my first "breech delivery". In the process, I gained considerable admiration for nurse and patient, and sympathy for the many new arrivals that come into the world under far more primitive conditions.

Some years later, Betty was still being called upon for assistance in deliveries. She was asked to accompany a pregnant lady, Iris Adjukak, on an emergency flight toYellowknife. It was mid-winter, and the plane was small. Betty had a premonition that all was not well, and packed a pair of scissors, a piece of string, newspapers, and Kleenex. All were needed over Great Bear Lake in the middle of the night! A little girl was born, and the pilot had to radio ahead to Yellowknife, announcing that an extra person had to be added to his passenger list! That little girl was later called "Angel", because, having arrived in our world from aloft in an airplane, she had "wings"!

Chapter 25

The Tongue of the People

For several centuries the reformed Anglican Communion has insisted upon ministering to the faithful in their own language. In the formative Thirty-nine Articles of 1562, Number 24 is entitled, "Of speaking in the congregation in such a tongue as the people understandeth." In the 1950s, no one was accepted into Arctic work that was not committed to learning the native languages. It was an essential.

However, with the Eskimo language, one faces a formidable barrier. Some may think that surely any primitive people who are clothed in the skins of animals, and who eat most of their food uncooked likely get along with a few well-placed guttural utter-

ABOVE: A song with the drum, obviously enjoyed. Alice Omadlak, ca. 1954.

ances and gesticulations. Nothing is further from the truth.

In actual fact, the Aleut-Eskimo language base has a most complicated structure. When its grammatical complexities are analysed in terms of the English language, we find it has, for example, nine cases of the noun. Whole sentences of complicated thought can be expressed in a single word of enormous length with a variety of suffixes, each placed in a precise order.

There are two ways to approach the task of learning this sophisticated language. You can study an approved grammar, but this was not available for the dialects in the Central Arctic. Or, you can learn from the people. I tried a bit of both, needing the grammatical foundation in order to grapple with the "building blocks" of the language for translation purposes.

In the early months of my ministry, I needed to use an interpreter for preaching in Church. This could be a frustrating exercise, especially when the interpreter knew what you were going to say.

A bilingual member of our congregation provided for me this illuminating "replay" after one sermon, as follows:

Sperry: "Today, I am going to talk about a boy named David."
Interpreter: "Today, he says, he is going to talk about the boy David, you know the one who looked after sheep and loved God."

Sperry: "David was a shepherd boy."
Interpreter: "Like I said, David looked after sheep."

Sperry: "David loved God."
Interpreter: "I said that; he loved God."

Sperry: "One day, David's father sent him on a journey."
Interpreter: "One day, he says, David's father sent him on a trip to visit his brothers in the war, and he's going to kill Goliath."

Small wonder that one worked for the day when one could do without the use of an interpreter.

Ethnographers call the language group in use throughout the Arctic "Eskimoid" or "Aleut-Eskimo". It is a group of related dialects used over one of the largest language areas in the world. When traditional subjects are being discussed, the spoken language can be understood by people from Alaska to Greenland.

Today, the language as spoken in Arctic Canada is called Inuktitut. The final suffix "-*tut*" simply means "like", or "similar" as "like the people". Inuktitut can be divided into several major and many minor dialects. In the central Arctic, the dialect spoken by the Copper Inuit (now being called the Kitengmiut, or the "people of the middle") is called *Inuinaktun*. It is an ancient form of the language, with some terms and pronunciations indicating that it may be an ancestral form to the dialects spoken to the east.

The people, especially the elders, are quite proud of their "own" dialects, and want others to know they have their own language. *Inuinaktun* is the tongue of the Central Arctic; *Inuvialuktun* is spoken west of the Coppermine River, into the Mackenzie Delta, and *Inupiatun* is spoken along the Alaskan arctic coast. However, the elders of these groups offer no objection to their languages simply being referred to as "Eskimo."

From Alaska to Greenland, the language of the people was never expressed in a written form until the arrival of the early missionaries. Those in Greenland, Labrador, Alaska, and in the western and central Canadian Arctic adopted a Roman, anglicized script, albeit with differing orthographies. In the eastern Canadian Arctic, however, a syllabic script was developed.

The development of Inuktitut syllabics was a direct result of the work of the Reverend James Evans, a Methodist missionary to the Crees in the 1840s. He adapted Pitman's Shorthand to express the various sounds of the Cree language in written form. The symbols were easily learned by those who spoke the language. This provided them with a way to record events and communicate over long distances. It provided the missionaries with a way to communicate the content of the Bible, hymns, and Christian teachings to far more people than they would be able to speak to directly. Later in the 1800s, Anglican Bishop Holden and the Reverend Edmund J. Peck adapted the system for the Inuit of northern Quebec and Baffin Island.

The system of syllabic usage was enormously successful. People fluent in Inuktitut could learn the writing system in about twenty-four hours of instruction and practice. Well into the 1900s, almost all the people living in the Eastern Arctic were literate in syllabic Inuktitut. Letters were exchanged between camps, and literature, including the New Testament, Book of Common Prayer, and hymnals, were being translated into Inuktitut. Today the use of the syllabic form of Inuktitut is one of three official languages (with English and French) of the new territory of Nunavut. It is, in fact, the official "working" language of the territory.

In the Central Arctic, the Anglican and Roman Catholic missionaries developed their own orthographies. This happened not because of any theological differences, but because of differing pronunciations following the Gallic or Anglo usage. Most Roman Catholic missionaries were of the Oblate order, from France or Belgium. Anglican missionaries were usually from England, Scotland, or southern Canada. But among the Inuinait themselves, once reading and writing came into general use, everyone spelled the words as they thought best. There was no standardized form.

Today, with the input of professional linguists and Inuit involved in teaching, efforts are being made to educate school students to spell according to one approved orthography. In the Central Arctic, the result of a decreasing use of their native language is that few students are able to use Inuinaktun in conversation, but can spell "correctly". On the other hand, the middle-aged and elders who can speak their language perfectly do not want to conform to the spelling of a modern orthography. They prefer to cling instead to the traditional practice of individual choice.

In addition, the use of Inuktitut syllabics is being encouraged throughout Nunavut. In the Kitikmeot, however, the elders do not understand syllabics (even if it is their own dialect written in syllabics). This further disassociates them from the language being used by government. It is a very real problem. With the 1999 creation of the new territory of Nunavut, and increased emphasis on Inuktitut as the official language, Inuinaktun is in danger of being forgotten. There are only three communities regarded as "Inuinait" and using their own dialect written in anglicised form. The overwhelming dominance of the eastern Inuktitut syllabic script and dialectic usage means that Inuinaktun as an historic dialect will be under enormous pressure of being absorbed into Inuktitut.

For many people, in those early years, the only books available for the Copper Inuinait were the few containing hymns, prayers, and selections from the Bible. However, in the 1950s, all these were in the dialects of the Western Arctic - that is, Inuvialuktun or Inupiatun. As I soon found out, these were poorly understood. This created an unusual dilemma for the clergy. Key words were often misunderstood. But among the people, that was not considered a problem. Instead, it added to the mystique. In their culture, mystery only added to the power.

It was not long ago that the shamans held sway with their powerful messages. When possessed by their helping spirits, the shamans offered oracles of uncertain meanings expressed in vocabularies not in common use. Contacts with the unseen did not require a clear understanding of the messages; these became all the more powerful for not being understood.

Even written words could be attributed as having special powers.

On our first furlough, I sent a postcard back to each of the families at Coppermine. One old gentleman, Adam Kaviyaktuk, always suffered from bad headaches. Upon my return, he expressed his deep gratitude for the powerful words I sent him on the card. He was having another severe headache when he received the card. He pressed the card against the painful area, he said, and the headache immediately disappeared.

Without disparaging the tendency to take everything literally, it was apparent that, to convey the meanings of the Scriptures to the people, translations would have to convey their meanings in the local context.

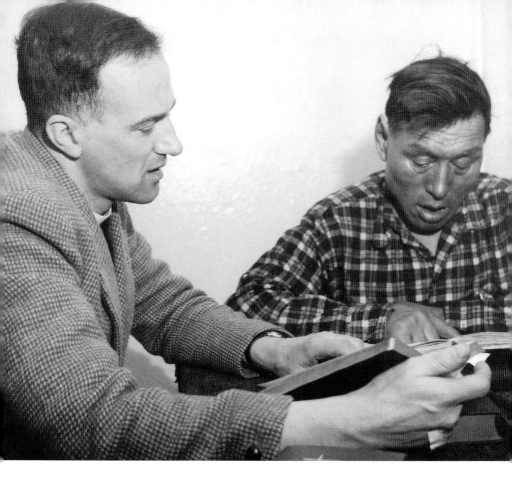

Chapter 26

"Write These Words"
Exodus 34:27

In the Christian Church, the Gospel has had a long tradition of oral transmission; the "Good News" being passed by the spoken word, through stories, song, and parables. Once the receiving people become literate in their own language, the written Word naturally followed. In some cases, there was no written language among the local people until a need for it was established. In the case of the Inuit, this was initially the need before the introduction of the Bible to these people.

The various ways of writing the "Eskimoid" languages (either syllabics or Roman orthography) were established by the missionary pioneers in various areas, based on personal preference. Roman

ABOVE: "So God does speak our language!" Alfred Okkaitok and Sperry, 1960s.

script was (and is) used exclusively by Lutherans in Greenland, Moravians in Labrador, and by Presbyterians or Episcopalians in Alaska. In Arctic Canada, the syllabic system was established throughout the eastern regions, in northern Quebec, in the Keewatin, and as far west as Cambridge Bay. From Cambridge Bay west, the Roman script was taught and is to this day preferred among the Kitengmiut, the Inuvialuit and on into Alaska.

The New Testament and parts of the Old Testament, translated into syllabic Inuktitut, had been available to the people of the Eastern Arctic for a good number of years. However, the "people in the middle", the Kitengmiut, did not read syllabics, and, their language, though similar, had enough differences and even in some instances, reversals of meaning, to make it essential to translate the Scriptures into their own dialect.

After working with the Kitengmiut for a number of years, and gaining proficiency in their language and a better understanding of their culture, I began to feel a compelling need to commence the task of Bible translation as soon as was practically possible.

Yet, the Scriptures and other ecclesiastical material should not be translated without careful adherence to the true meaning of the source text. Otherwise, clear understanding would be difficult, and any integrity would be lost. Today, scholars of the ancient languages of the Bible provide crucial advice and checks on all current translations, ensuring as much accuracy as is possible.

The translation teams of the United Bible Societies all over the world have long worked under such discipline. However, in my earlier years in the Arctic, the centre for such operations was the headquarters of the British and Foreign Bible Society in London, England. Prior to the publishing of any manuscript by the Canadian Bible Society, it was necessary to provide evidence that we had a sufficient grasp of the language and culture of the people. Of course, it was also necessary to ensure that the people themselves had expressed a keen desire to have God's Word written in their own dialect. Of that, there was no question.

In the Arctic, translations had been done some years previously in a western dialect for the Anglican Book of Common Prayer and a few hymns. However, these lacked the necessary checks and balances required by today's standards. The task was daunting, but would enhance people's understanding, and also provide widely scattered communities with a common book, which records the very foundation of the Christian faith. Additionally, it provided further stimulation among the people towards literacy, with wider possibilities for better communication within their society, and a way of preserving their own stories, as well.

Eventually, with full approval of the Canadian Bible Society, which was sponsoring the Scripture translations for the Central Arctic, the project began.

Some of the problems that faced us bordered on the comical.

From a cultural aspect, there can be no greater background contrast than that between the ancient lifestyles of the people of the agricultural Middle East than that of the hunting people of the Arctic regions. Special study and insight were required, tested at every level by the closest cooperation with local informants, whose input was invaluable. Modern Bible translators have long accepted the principle of "dynamic equivalence". This means that the inner meaning of the text must be expressed in a way that made sense to the local people, rather than relying on literal translation alone.

Throughout the process, some help was available in the form of biblical texts from other translations: Alaskan Inupiat, Eastern Arctic syllabics, Labrador Eskimo, and Greenlandic. But our people were really awaiting the words of a God who spoke in their own familiar dialect, or as they said, "the language of our hearts".

The Arctic people were historically "godless", having no concept of a single supreme divine being. How do you introduce such an unknown being?

A century ago, an early Alaskan missionary attempted to find the answer by asking who was the most important person in the village. He was told it was the "*Umialik*"- the owner of the *umiak*. The *umiak* is a large skin boat used on the ocean to transport whole families, their dogs, and gear in the summer, and is vital to the survival of the group. Accepting this, an early translation of the Lord's Prayer began, "Umialikput kilangmiitutin...." or "Our Boat-owner, who is in heaven...." Eventually, the word "God" replaced "boat-owner" as an introduced and learned concept.

Some very obvious cultural usages have always found their way into the various texts of every regional Bible translation. A good example is from the Lord's Prayer. The request for daily "bread" has always been translated "meat" simply because the flesh either of animals or fish was the only food available. However, today, the word for meat, neki, applies to food of every description.

Also confusing are instances when an animal is used as a metaphor, particularly if the same species is common in the Arctic. In Luke l3: 32, Jesus refers to King Herod as "that fox". With the great variety of foxes in the Arctic, and the importance of this animal to the people, the question arises: Which of our various varieties is closest to the Palestinian example? Including seasonal phases of their coats, we have foxes that are, white, red, silver, cross and blue. Quite a variety, but all are fairly harmless and only a threat to lemmings! Truly, the Arctic fox can hardly be considered a sinister menace.

Obviously, Jesus' characterization of Herod as a "fox" had little to do with an inoffensive nature. That king was a vicious, vindictive, cunning monster greatly feared by all his subjects. The nearest animal we have that might come closest to that description is the largest member of the weasel family, the wolverine. The wolverine is not large but has a proven reputation as being unusually strong for its size, cunning, and, when cornered, particularly vicious. After consultation with our team, we decided that the wolverine was obviously the right animal to characterize Herod.

Incidentally, when Jesus referred (in another place in Scripture) to foxes having their dens, their characteristics are of no concern so we made them red foxes, as close to the colour of their Palestinian "cousin" as possible.

Jonah's "whale" was also a problem in translation; a number of species of whales reside in Arctic waters. While these large mammals are well known to the people, their ability to swallow human beings is uncertain. Allegedly, however, in our large lakes to the south lives a very large fish called an *ikaluakpak*, a huge fish. This monster fish has the reputation of being able to swallow small herds of swimming caribou and to pursue hunters in their kayaks!

Ikaluakpak is so entrenched in the folklore of the people that we chanced the suggestion that the term for this "great fish" might be used to represent the animal that swallowed Jonah in the text of Holy Scripture. Of course, predictably, the consultants in London reminded me that we translators must be faithful to historical fact without any flirtations with mythology. They asked, "Did the people really believe there was an *ikaluakpak*?"

Of course they did. Most folk had distant relatives who have been swallowed by one and the wake of such a beast is frequently seen speeding across lakes to this day. So this huge fish was authorized accordingly.

Conversely, the translation of any action that lacks obvious parallels in the local setting must be dealt with carefully, as it presents special problems. For instance, when Jesus promised to make his followers "fishers of men'", we could not use words that conveyed the actual use of a net or fish spear. The meaning had to be "seeking", with good intentions. For that, the language had an obvious suffix: *-hiuk-*. This tucks into a word and conveys the meaning "looking for". It is particularly used when hunting for animals.

Consequently, it seemed obvious that I could use a combination meaning, "I will make you to become those who will search for people" (*Inukhiuktinguktitauniaktuhi*). I usually consulted the elders in the community for these matters, and in this instance, I was certainly glad I did! I was given a stern warning NOT to use this word. The elders spoke of their early years and the use of -hiuk-. According to them, if this is applied to a human being, it means the hunter is to kill and take revenge for the murder committed against a relative, a sort of vendetta practice. Chastened, I left the problem for further enlightenment.

Some time afterwards, there was a tragedy in the community involving a young couple. These young people were traveling by dogteam from a community about a hundred and twenty miles northwest of Coppermine. It was wintertime and the man was not an experienced traveler but was following the trail of other teams, which had come the same way. While they were en route, a blizzard developed, and they lost the trail. Unwisely, the young man left the dogs, the sled, and his partner to search for other tracks. He was never seen again.

With a head wind to guide them, the dogs themselves came into Coppermine (the scent of a community will carry for miles for dogs) and the distracted woman arrived with no man. After a day or two, and improved weather, a search was organized. During the carrying out of the search, I distinctly heard one young man call out to another, "Inukhiungnialekutin akagu?" (Are you going man-hunting tomorrow?)

Obviously, the intent here was to save a life, not destroy it. Further checking showed that some of the terms used by the elders had, over the years and under the influence of a new way of life, been radically changed for the better. So the words of our Lord could be translated with a modern meaning for the benefit of all. We adopted the use of -*hiuk*-, grateful for its modern and current understanding.

Chapter 27

Stories

Stories were told and retold during long winter evenings in the iglus. This was entertainment, education, and the way information was saved and passed from generation to generation. In those old days, the children were happy participants in these activities, listening for the most part intently, and learning the stories through the telling and retelling.

I heard hundreds of stories during my half-century in the North. Some of these had obviously been retold many times. Others were more recent, often accounts of observed happenings.

Among the Inuinait there is an absence of any stories that suggest an understanding of traceable history; none that I know of refer

ABOVE: Arctic veteran of many winters. Photo: M.J. Hewitt.

to the early migrations from the west. More often the stories reflect mythological relationships between humans and animals and their encounters, and how the animals came to have their appendages and current appearances.

I kept a record of some of the stories and the people who told them. These are a few, recounted from my papers.

The Loon and the Raven
Told by Illattiak, the famous shaman from Bathurst Inlet

The yellow-billed loon once met the raven. They talked together and the raven tattooed the loon, putting streaks on it and painting its bill yellow. Then it asked the loon to paint it in turn, but the loon threw lamp soot all over it. The raven was white before but afterward it was black.

The Lazy Hunter
Told by Alfred Okkaituk

One summer inland, each day all the men went walking in different directions looking for caribou. Because the ground was rocky they quickly wore out the skin soles on their boots and the women had to sew fresh patches on them every evening. Whilst most men were occasionally successful in the hunt, one man never seemed even to see caribou although he returned with the soles of his boots worn through.

Since he was not a successful hunter, no woman would stay with him. Finally, one woman felt sorry for him and moved into his tent. Still, he had no success, and the woman began to be suspicious. She followed him the next day to see what he did. Sure enough, away from the camp, he climbed down into a small valley in which was a sharp rock sticking up. There she saw him lying back on the mossy ground rubbing his boots up and down over the rock's sharp edge to give the appearance of wearing out. That was enough; she left him and the lazy hunter was alone once more.

Returned from the Dead
Told by Alfred Okkaituk

There are many stories about people being raised from the dead, and, the people say, shamans often died and came back to life again. Once, far towards the east, an old man died in the winter. The family took his body, wrapped it in caribou skins and left him on a nearby hill. Later that night, the old man came back alive and sat with his family in the snowhouse. Very soon, though, he got very tired and died all over again.

The Jealous Kayaker
Told by Ikey Bolt

There was once, at Bathurst Inlet, a woman who had two husbands. The three seemed to get on well together.

One day in the summer the two men went caribou hunting to a small island. One man paddled the kayak while the other lay on his stomach on the front with his bow and arrows. When the kayak reached the shore the front man jumped off with his weapons, expecting to be followed. However, the paddler, who was really jealous about the woman, took off and marooned his partner on the island.

The abandoned hunter did manage to kill a caribou as well as many Arctic hare. He made clothing for himself from their skins. Somehow he survived all that summer and into the fall until the sea froze over.

Finally, he was able to walk over the ice and arrived at the people's camp where they were already living in snowhouses. He arrived in the dark when the people were gathered in the large dance-house. In those days anyone with a special song or story could take the drum.

Dressed in his strange rabbitskin clothing, in walked the man everyone thought had been dead for weeks. Taking the drum and standing directly before the man who abandoned him, he began a lament for one who was left to die, accompanying his song with the booming beating of the drum.

The shameful story unfolded in the song. Finally the culprit could stand it no longer. Bowing his head on his chest, he left the snowhouse, took his dogs and was never seen again.

Breathing Under Water
Told by Ikey Bolt

Every winter the men always hunted seals on the ice. Dogs who could smell well would guide them to the breathing holes, which are carved through the ice from under the water by the seal's flippers.

The hunter would wait, sometimes for hours, until the seal came up to breathe. When an indicator stick, stuck into the hole under the snow, started to move up it meant the seal was coming up to breathe.

Then the hunter plunges his harpoon downward to hit the seal. The harpoon head, attached to a long thong, buries itself into the seal and as it tries to swim away, the hunter holds on to the line to drag it back and up on to the ice surface.

The unknown factor is what kind of seal has been harpooned. Most are the smaller ringed seals, which a hunter can handle by himself. But, the square flipper or bearded seal is much larger, and, if caught, requires the assistance of other hunters to drag it upon the ice. An additional danger is that if the harpooner, upon getting a strike, wraps the line with the wrong hitch round his wrist. Then, the bearded seal can become the "hunter" and the unfortunate man the victim!

There was this man seal hunting south of Ukalik Islands and he harpooned a square flipper. He could tell by the strong pull on his line that he needed much help and called out to other hunters. Whilst doing so he made a turn on his wrist with the line; but it was not done in a way that, if necessary, it could slip off. So the large seal dragged the poor man down the breathing hole and under the ice.

But while he was being towed under the water, as the story goes, he remembered that there was a pocket of air under his armpit. From that spot he was able to draw a breath. The big seal then came up for a breath at another hole where another hunter was waiting. Again a harpoon came down, striking the seal. This time, other men joined the hunter and, together, they dragged the seal to the surface of the ice. To their amazement, after it on another line, followed the man who had been breathing from his armpit, but, by that time, he had almost run out of air!

After each hunt, journey or other experience, stories would be shared and impressions related. Not everyone was in agreement even as to what minor taboos should be followed; these differed from one area to another.

One afternoon during a round of visiting in Coppermine, following my custom, I included visits to the elders. Two old men, who were boys before southern influences arrived, were always happy to have an interested listener. The topic of caribou hunting was always popular and, in the first home, I was informed that if you are hunting in the fall, during the rut, sometimes you come across two fighting bulls with their antlers interlocked.

In order to kill both, you take your mitts off, fold one and tuck it into the other and lay them on the ground. Then you approach the bulls and can easily kill them both with your knife; they can't get free if your mitts are likewise "stuck" together.

Intrigued by this information, I thought I'd gain additional understanding of the story by repeating it next door where the second old gentleman lived, a veteran of as many hunts as the first. This elder informed me that he had never heard anything like that in his life and dismissed it out of hand!

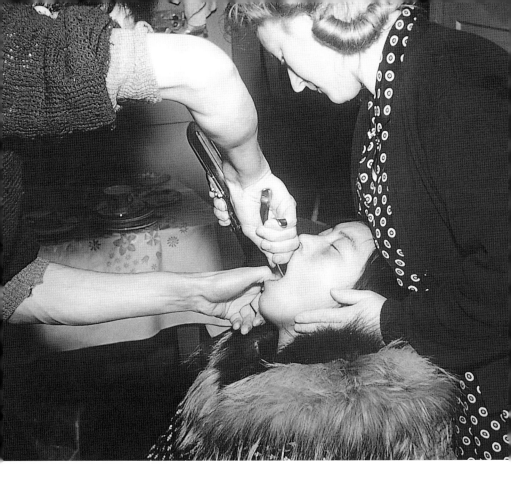

Chapter 28

Heal the Sick

Long ago, the lives of the Inuit in those distant hunting camps included times of plenty and contentment despite the uncertainties of life in general in such a harsh environment. However, when sickness strikes, a snowhouse or a tent is not the most desirable place to be.

Traditionally, in their culture, any kind of sickness or accident demanded a reason. Invariably, the root cause would be deemed to be the malicious attack of a malignant spirit or due to the breaking of a taboo. The shaman would be called in for assistance and, depending on his powers to defeat the evil influence, his prestige would be enhanced or diminished. The people of this part of the

ABOVE: Part of the job, providing dental care to the people.
Pulling teeth – Sperry, Betty Sperry assisting.

Arctic were generally not familiar with medicinal remedies from plants or roots, so their options were very limited.

One entrenched practice was to attempt to evict the sickness or weakness by renaming the victim. This was especially common in dealing with illness in young children. By renaming the patient the parents thought the malady would leave the body, together with the child's persona. Once given a new name, a new lease on life is possible. This understanding is somewhat in the same category as naming a newborn infant after the last family member to die before the new arrival; it carried with it a vague idea of reincarnation. Even today, name-changing for weak or sickly infants still continues in some circles, especially when elders, who remember the old traditions, exert their influence.

The early missionaries brought varying levels of medical knowledge to the healing of the sick. Some were fairly highly trained, and others had little formal training. My predecessor at Coppermine, Harold Webster, took a year off from his mission to study medicine at Livingstone College in London, England. Inspired by the need he saw every day; he enrolled in a course designed for missionaries working in various parts of the world.

In the Coppermine mission house, we had a modest supply of medicines. Prior to the establishment of a nursing station staffed by a health professional; the medicines here were replenished by the government each year. In the days before the Territorial Government assumed responsibility for the delivery of medical services, others besides the missionaries also did what they could to deal with sickness and accidents in the Arctic communities. Members of the Royal Canadian Mounted Police and traders operating the posts for the Hudson's Bay Company were particularly helpful to the people in times of sickness or accidents.

But it was the two missions, Anglican and Roman Catholic, who actually established and maintained hospitals in the Arctic. These were sponsored and financially supported by the Government of Canada. The healing ministry was offered for a good number of years; the Government finally took over administration and staffing for all hospital services in the 1960s.

In recent years it is a fact that Christian mission work has undergone close scrutiny in regard to its motivation and operations, at least by some sections of the aboriginal community. However, to date there has been nothing but appreciation for the healing ministry, including the self-sacrificing labours of doctors, nurses and other staff who gave time and skills for the relief of suffering over the years. This dedication is still well remembered by the elders across the entire North.

The enormous need for healing services was never in question. Unfortunately, many diseases accompanied outsiders into the isolation of the Arctic, and spread like wildfire through the indigenous populations. The entire history of European exploration and occupation in the Americas is peppered with stories of unintentional introduction of lethal epidemics, which decimated many aboriginal populations. Europeans and American colonists had built up a resistance to many diseases such as diphtheria, measles, polio, scarlet fever, mumps, whooping cough, influenza, tuberculosis, and sexually transmitted diseases. The people they came into contact with in the North had no such resistance.

In the 1940s and 1950s, the main concern in our Arctic communities was the scourge of tuberculosis.

In its concern for the health of the northern people, the federal government began to establish small nursing stations in the larger settlements in the late forties. Eventually, yearly X-ray surveys were performed at every trading post. In the Eastern Arctic, teams brought in by ship conducted these. In the west the X-ray aircraft transported units and technicians. A team of doctors accompanied the survey teams and word was sent to outside camps to bring all the families in for the occasion.

The government encouraged cooperation in these surveys by promising dogfeed supplies for the hundreds of dogs that would transport the families in to the posts. These dogs would need feeding until they could return to their camps, where their normal food was cached or readily available by hunting. Once the tests were set up, all of us in the settlement agencies were recruited to give assistance, especially in identifying individuals. This could be difficult for those who did not know the local people.

The Inuit way of bestowing names did not rely on "family names". In other words, each person might have one or more names, but there was no name common to an entire family, such as surnames. As in southern society, some unrelated individuals bear the same name, which adds to the confusion. For some years now, the system of regularizing registrations of families has resulted in all members of each family taking the name of its head as a "last" name or surname.

As government services, including health and education services, increased, there was a need to be able to identify individuals, so that records could be kept. Before paternalistic family names were bestowed upon the Inuit, each person was assigned a number. For outside health officials, it was all very confusing to sort out unless one knew the families intimately. However, most people cooperated obligingly, and readily offered their "disc numbers".

Unfortunately, the entire X-ray survey conveyed to the people a sense of uncertainty as that mysterious machine appeared to be able to "read" the state of one's lungs and might be a source of bad news. The plates were read each evening by competent physicians and the verdict announced without delay.

In the Western Arctic, all who were suspected of having contracted tuberculosis were flown out to the Charles Camsell Hospital in Edmonton, Alberta. Hospitalization caused a long period of separation from family and loved ones, but was generally accepted courageously, though with heart-wrenching "good-byes" and many a tear.

Once a week, if radio reception was good, a doctor from the southern hospital would read out the names of patients and would report their condition. Consequently, all contact was not lost with the loved ones in the south, although the absence of confidentiality would never be acceptable today. In the church on Sunday afternoons, I would tape messages from families so that the patients themselves could hear their voices, news, and greetings.

Despite all the efforts to increase health services, immunity against foreign diseases was still very difficult to establish. In Coppermine, we experienced an outbreak of German measles in 1952, Asian flu and red measles in 1957, and a terrible influenza outbreak in 1960. At such times, the medical services of the government responded as speedily and efficiently as possible to help quell the outbreak and save lives.

In our experience, Northern nurses were superb, particularly before modern communications were available. They had to understand the people, even if the people were not able to really communicate what was wrong. They often had to diagnose and treat patients without the benefit of a physician's opinion, especially if radio reception was poor at the time.

In my memory, the epidemics of 1957 and 1960 were the most devastating. These particular "bugs" traveled through the population with terrifying speed. Once one or two people fell sick, within days literally everyone else was also sick. The school building became a hospital, filled with patients bedded down on the floor throughout. The real problem lay in the fact that these "white men's diseases" might affect Euro-Canadians only slightly, yet be devastating or fatal in their effect on the aboriginal people of the North.

In their homes, still pretty primitive by today's standards, the affected people lay on their beds, most too sick to attend to their own physical needs. Meanwhile, along the shore, hundreds of dogs still needed to be fed. I recall one brave RCMP constable, though unwell himself, gallantly cooking dog food for his own team and trying to meet the needs of many additional dogs. This type of emergency seems to bring out the very best in so many.

In such situations, those of us who seemed to have immunity to the disease were thankful to be spared the illness affecting so many of our friends and neighbours. There were few of us in the "immune" category; most people did become ill.

For our family, with the usual reliable baby-sitters also down with the illness, Betty was housebound with our two small children. She undertook the task of cooking and feeding all the extra nursing staff flown in to help deal with the emergency, for which they were most grateful.

During an outbreak, those who could do so acted as interpreters for the doctor, and often served in the bedpan "ministry", emptying bedpans and in general trying to ensure cleanliness. In addition, those of us in the clergy offered pastoral support for the worried and harassed patients who could hardly help themselves, let alone their children.

Worst of all was the duty of having to remove the dead and then having to break the news to desperately ill relatives who were in no state to receive such news. Also, in the crowded situation of an epidemic, both the disease and sad tidings traveled like wildfire, leaving many not only weakened, but also deeply bereaved.

Renate Wilson's book, *Thank God and Dr. Cass* (published in 1989) tells a more detailed story of the 1960 epidemic, and the role of Dr. Elizabeth Cass in dealing with the illness. Dr. Cass was an opthalmologist with wide medical experience who happened to be working in Coppemine at the time of the 1960 outbreak of influenza.

In the last thirty years, due to immunization programs and naturally acquired immunity, the epidemics have decreased, although RSV (Respiratory Syncychial Virus) is still a problem among infants and young children throughout Nunavut.

Today, many of the people of the Arctic have apparently joined the mainstream of Canadian life with maladies hardly heard of in those former years - cancer, arthritis, obesity, AIDS and related immune deficiency diseases. Energetic programs are introduced to encourage healthy lifestyles, especially for pregnant women. However, problems related to smoking, alcohol, and unhealthy "junk food" diets are more common now than in the 1950s, manifesting themselves as alcoholism and related liver problems, diabetes, and increased rates of asthma, emphysema, and allergies.

Today, our Arctic communities for the most part have well-equipped health centres staffed with a combination of nurse-practitioners, licensed nurses, local health workers, and doctors who stay in the community for varying periods of time. Some communities, such as Rankin Inlet, have developed successful birthing centres staffed in part by Inuit midwives. However, it is still difficult to attract health care professionals, especially doctors and nurses, to the North. Recruitment and keeping professionals in the community require constant vigilance.

Though the era of mission hospitals is long gone, the ministry of the Church remains, proclaiming a Gospel that includes a call for whole and healthy lifestyles reflective of an inner commitment of faith and obedience to God.

Chapter 29

"Teach the Children"
Leviticus 16:11

Along with the care and healing of the sick, a parallel Christian concern has always been that of education. For many centuries the Church has been a major influence in both fields. Worldwide, educational initiatives have not always been either approved or encouraged by secular rulers who felt far less threatened by subjects who were illiterate and, consequently, unquestioning about what was happening in the wide world beyond their village.

So, in a special sense, with the arrival of explorers, traders and missionaries, the door to a new world opened for the people of the Arctic. There was immediate delight and interest in the products of technology the newcomers brought with them. Steel needles,

ABOVE: Cultural activities in school, ca. 1955. Kathy Kimpton, teacher.

colourful fabrics, buttons, metal cookware, rifles, nails and tools, flour, tea.... All were immediately embraced.

Notwithstanding, we of the Anglican mission, with its evangelistic mandate and disinterest in trading commerce, were primarily concerned with understanding both the language and the culture of the people we felt called to serve.

In those days the missions insisted on language efficiency for all its missionaries. This had to be acquired by serious study and frequent visitations to distant hunting camps. Throughout the Diocese, the Church never concluded that a response to the Gospel would be stronger if everyone learned English.

Recent accusations that the mission of the Church was to obliterate aboriginal culture and languages conveniently seem to ignore the historical fact that the many languages used by the First Nations in Canada were adapted to written form under the direct influence of early missionaries. Rev. James Evans' invention of the syllabic writing system for the Cree people was an excellent example of this. Far from obliterating a culture, the newfound ability to capture stories in written form encouraged the preservation of culture and languages.

However, across the North, as contacts with southern influences increased, a new concern surfaced. Particularly in the Western Arctic, the people themselves became convinced that, in order to "hold their own" and do business with the newcomers (and they were doing significant business, in trading furs), some knowledge of their language would be useful. Many Alaskan Inupiat moved into the Mackenzie Delta in the early 1900s. Most were able to speak and understand English, and their ability to communicate with the traders demonstrated the usefulness of that faculty to the local people along the Arctic coast.

Consequently, in the Western Arctic and along the Mackenzie River, both the Roman Catholic and Anglican Churches established schools. An Anglican school was established in 1908 at Hay River in the upper Mackenzie region. This school accepted students from the entire length of the Mackenzie Valley. In l929, a modest school was established on the Arctic coast at Shingle Point, west of the Mackenzie Delta. Later, in l937, All Saints' Anglican Residential School was built and operated at Aklavik in the western delta. This school was later expanded in the new town of Inuvik.

Only a few young people from the Central Arctic attended the schools at Shingle Point, Aklavik, (and later) Inuvik. However, as adults, I knew all these people very well indeed, and could communicate with them both in English and in their mother tongue, which each had retained, without exception. From the countless stories they told of their schooldays, I was able to form impressions that have stayed with me ever since. Most of the stories and impressions are certainly in marked contrast with the more recently reported horrific accounts of life in southern residential schools operated by churches and sponsored by the Government of Canada.

From the frank witness of ex-students of the Anglican schools mentioned above, common threads emerge. Each readily admitted something of the trauma they felt in leaving home for a distant place they had never seen before. Their parents, they said, convinced them that it would be good for them and their people if they could learn the language of the white man. Not one of these people ever suggested that they were "taken" either by persuasion or force by the Government or their agencies. In any case, at that time the Royal Canadian Mounted Police represented the Government in the Arctic and forcing children to go unwillingly to distant schools was not a part of their mandate. It simply was not done.

Still, as early as the middle 1950s there was increasing concern about the length of time children going to school were separated from their parents and the home environment. For an experimental few years, the Government established a tent hostel at Coppermine, which was administered by the Anglican Church. This hostel operated from April until August, housing the children from various camps while they attended school in the community. The concept was that a shorter period away from home would not rob them of their traditional lifestyle and culture, while still allowing them to obtain part of the education offered to children in the rest of Canada.

My responsibility in the establishment of the tent hostel was to visit the camps, describe the initiative, and talk with the parents about it, to determine if they were interested. In the exercise of these duties, I learned how stringent the government procedures were in ensuring that the parents were fully advised. It was ONLY with their approval and permission that children could be accepted for the hostel and school.

The tent hostel operated for four spring and summer seasons. Approximately thirty children were accommodated each year. The staff largely consisted of local Inuit, chosen especially for their interest in the welfare of the children. All were able, and encouraged, to communicate with the children in their own language. The children attending school in this program had many opportunities to interact with the local boys and girls. They, including our two children, all played together and took joint classes in the school in Coppermine.

Although this program was successful, most parents told us that they preferred a longer school year for their children. This increasingly became possible as more families moved into the communities. Within a few years, local schools were built in many of the smaller settlements, and the children no longer came to Coppermine. However, while it lasted, the Coppermine tent hostel introduced the children to their first steps in formal education.

The current torrent of criticism of Church-run residential schools in the south is somewhat bewildering to those of us who lived in the Western and Central Arctic at the time. The blanket condemnation of residential schools saddens those of us who worked with schools in the North.

Apologies from Church authorities contain only the barest recognition of the sacrificial and compassionate service a whole generation of good and trusted supervisors and teachers offered for so many years in the past.

Whilst the earlier system, in which children were sent to school with little chance of returning home for months or even years, is rightly to be deplored, at least it shows the determination of their parents to accept such a separation for the sake of their children's education. The legacy of such obvious sacrifice was that a number of young adults finally returned home equipped and skilled in preparation for leadership in their communities, and for the changing world that awaited them. Many of these are the aboriginal leaders of today, nationally as well as throughout the North.

In my more recent travels in the Western Arctic, I have often spoken with elders and adults who attended residential schools. In their memories, willingly recounted to me, they recall some supervisors and teachers with more affection than others, but ill treatment or various categories of abuse are never mentioned. One can only assume that, generally, the staff, true to their Christian calling, cared for their charges and truly earned the respect for which they have been remembered.

Reverend Leonard and Mrs. Dorothy Holman, for instance, superintendents at Aklavik and then Stringer Hall, in Inuvik, established a record for integrity and loving care for their charges without parallel. They, and so many others, deserve the thanks and approbation of the Church if only to match the gratitude of the hundreds of students who still recall their hostel caregivers with the highest regard and affection.

Chapter 30

Winds of Change

The long history of the Canadian Arctic has been one of constant (and sometimes dramatic) change. Even in the last half of the twentieth century, there have been major environmental and societal changes in the circumpolar Arctic. Some of these are sinister indeed, due to their complex origins and widespread effects.

The ecology of the Arctic is so very fragile that uncontrolled exploration and development have always caused deep concern. That concern, in my opinion, has not been ignored by major corporations, which have instituted their own internal disciplines, monitored by a watchful government.

In former times, the local people lived in fear of the unseen world

ABOVE: Caribou (tuktu) are an essential component of the life of the Inuinait, even today. Photo: Page Burt.

of spirit-powers and shades of the dead. More recently, the threat of major pollution of air, land and sea has largely taken their place. The danger to the caribou herds is a good example of problems caused by pollution on a world scale. It is an established fact that radiation fallout due to atmospheric nuclear testing has seriously affected lichens throughout the Arctic. In addition, aerial dispersion of PCBs throughout the northern hemisphere has also affected food chains across the Arctic. A third major problem is thinning of the ozone layer over the Arctic and Antarctic regions, due to greenhouse gases circulating in the upper atmosphere.

These problems in turn affect the climate, plants, and the major food preference of many Arctic people - the caribou.

Had not nuclear testing been terminated by formal international agreements, one can imagine similar consequences for northern caribou as those experienced after the Chernobyl nuclear disaster in the Ukraine. In that incident, winds blew the radiation fallout into northern Scandinavia. This affected the reindeer of the Laplanders, resulting in entire herds being slaughtered after consuming radioactive-poisoned tundra vegetation.

PCB buildup in the fat and muscle tissue of sea mammals and caribou due to the biological magnification of chemicals through the food chain offers long-term threats to the well being of people who depend on these animals for food.

The thinning of the ozone layer contributes to global warming, concentrating the warming effects in polar latitudes. There has been a measurable increase in the average year round temperature of the Arctic over the past twenty years, and many scientists think this increase will accelerate.

Of course, caribou can also suffer from local natural disasters, one of which might be better understood after the experience of the people of Quebec and parts of Ontario in 1998. During their momentous ice storm, huge tracts of maple forest were destroyed, tens of thousands of branches smashed from trees in urban areas, and several million people were without electrical power for long periods.

Ice plays a frightening part in Arctic perils. Particularly in the fall, after freeze-up, a temporary thaw with rain may be followed by hard freezing before the moisture evaporates. If this happens, a hardened crust of ice encases the plants upon which the caribou and musk oxen feed. If this icing is followed by a snowfall, the problem is magnified. Caribou are particularly vulnerable. Deep snow on top of an ice crust renders their food supply inaccessible. Caribou paw to uncover the vegetation on which they feed. If they cannot break through the snow and icy crust with their hoofs, starvation can result. At the very minimum, this causes the caribou to have to move long distances to suitable snow, a further drain on their fat reserves in the early part of the winter. The results of this are not immediately seen; cows may abort or resorb fetuses, or starvation may strike later in the winter.

Scientists fear that the increase in fall thaws and freezing rain in the High Arctic, as well as an increase in the instability of the Arctic weather systems, have in part been factors contributing to the serious decline of the Peary caribou in the High Arctic.

The effects of global warming on caribou are complex and frightening. According to scientists like Dr. Anne Gunn, working in the Arctic, warm summers and early springs mean that the vegetation will "green-up" earlier, placing the time of peak nutrients prior to the time when the caribou need them most. Warmer summers may mean as much as a 13% increase in mosquito populations in the Barrenlands, causing caribou to have to move about more frequently, and decreasing the time they can spend grazing, sending them into the breeding season too thin to conceive. Internal parasite loads can increase; stomach parasites cause loss of appetite in caribou, again sending them into the breeding season in a condition that prevents conception.

Warmer winters affect migration; delayed freeze-up may cause herds like the Dolphin-Union herd to take unnecessary chances on the thin ice of the Dolphin and Union Straits, or may delay their leaving Victoria Island, causing overgrazing of the staging areas along the coast of the island and subsequent poor condition in animals on those ranges.

Not all populations of a given species are threatened with serious depletion. During the 1950s, that resolute survivor of the Ice Age, the musk ox, was an extreme rarity, due to decades of overhunting throughout the Arctic. Even in areas where they were once plentiful, many native people grew to old age without ever seeing one.

However, beginning with the establishment of the Thelon Game Sanctuary in 1927, measures were taken to protect the musk ox throughout the Arctic. Hunting was prohibited in some places except in emergencies, and quotas were established in other places. In addition, large predators were killed off over large areas of musk ox range, not specifically to protect the musk oxen, but as a general effort to reduce the populations of predators.

In recent years, musk ox have increased at an alarming rate in areas where predators were decimated, particularly on Banks Island in the western Arctic, where the present population is estimated at well over eighty thousand. This has alarming consequences for the local people. Alarming, because high populations of musk oxen cause the animals to widen their selection of forage, forcing them into competition with the caribou for food. When musk oxen are abundant, the caribou seem to move elsewhere. The meat of the caribou is strongly preferred by the local people, and in places on Banks and western Victoria Islands, they are unfortunately becoming less accessible.

At the same time, musk ox populations on the mainland have not kept pace with the increases seen on Banks and Victoria Islands. It is thought that two factors affect this - the presence of far more predators, in particular the grizzly bear, and the presence of a lungworm parasite in the musk ox population. In the area to the southeast of Kugluktuk, it is rare to see a herd of musk oxen with more than one or two calves after the end of May. It is quite likely most are taken by wolves or bears. Grizzlies can and do prey on adult musk oxen also.

Populations of wildlife are never static. Vole and lemming populations occur in cycles, great abundance some years, cycling to low populations in others. Lemmings and voles are the main diet of Arctic and red foxes, so the fox cycle follows that of the voles and lemmings. Snowy owls also depend on the little rodents, so their population cycle echoes the lemming cycle.

Wolves follow the caribou and provide an unending argument among northerners about their usefulness. It is true that they do cull the caribou herds by pulling down the old and sick but, in some areas, have a great killing spree with newborn calves. However, this in itself is a part of the natural web of life. The caribou produce far more calves than the environment can support if all calves grew to maturity. Since caribou cows have virtually no way of defending their young, they all calve at the same time, "flooding the market" with protein (in the way of vulnerable calves). The local wolves take all they can in a short period of time. The calves grow quickly, and are able to follow their mothers in hours, able to keep up with a herd within a week.

In the heyday of trapping, wolves were considered a destructive enemy of the trapper. A wolf might follow the tracks of a trapper working his line, killing every trapped fox. There was such an outcry from the trappers about wolf-kills that, for a time, the Government sanctioned the setting of poisoned bait. That policy didn't last for long as other carnivores took the same bait and died, and the main purpose was ineffectual.

The wolf is truly a noble animal. In a pack, only the alpha male and female breed, yet most members seem to care for the young. Wolves are powerful hunters but, like most large predators, have trouble bringing down healthy adult caribou. But then, in the Arctic a natural death for any animal is almost unknown. When any animal becomes weakened, it is usually taken by predators. It is a case of "nature red in tooth and claw." This is the way of the wild.

Chapter 31

The Reasons Why

Changes affecting life in the North in our generation have been profound. Some of these were gradual, and a result of increased attention from "Outside"; others were stimulated by significant events
elsewhere in the world.

One technological advance that dramatically altered the lives of
the scattered population of the Arctic was the airplane. These were
described in most dialects, appropriately, as "*tingmiak*", the bird. In
earlier days, for the most part, isolated settlements had to rely on
communications in winter by dogsled, and in summer, if the sea
was calm enough, by freighter canoe for short journeys. Mail delivery was uncertain and necessary evacuation for the sick was fraught

ABOVE: The airplane became central to the development of the North.
Hercules aircraft on an ice strip at Coppermine (Kugluktuk).

with perils. For the Kitengmiut, once the DEW Line was in operation, Coppermine was the northern extremity of the air travel network, and Cambridge Bay became the eastern limit, Throughout the fifties, most trading posts had no scheduled flights whatsoever; there was just an occasional visit by a charter or company plane. Both the RCMP and the Hudson's Bay Company had their own aircraft; the latter made a yearly inspection visit for the Hudson's Bay Company.

Bishop Marsh chartered an aircraft for his yearly pastoral visits, and I occasionally accompanied him on these trips. He chartered veteran bush pilots - Brock (Rocky) Parsons with his Norseman from Churchill, or Bob Engle with his Beaver from Yellowknife.

Various aircraft companies served these small northern destinations, but the credit for an expansion that closed those community gaps certainly needs to go to Bob Engle and his expanding fleet of DC-3s, under the Northwest Territorial Air banner. He initiated scheduled north-south flights to Holman, and east-west flights that linked the Arctic Coast communities as far east as Spence Bay (now called Taloyoak).

The North owes much to these pioneers of aviation. Flying conditions were at times incredibly harsh, and the pilots were forced to work under considerable hardship. However, they created and maintained regular supply routes, brought speedy relief for the sick, and fostered face-to-face meetings among people who otherwise never would have met. Scheduled air transport also provided a means by which visiting opportunities were substantially increased for the scattered family groups across the Arctic. This was important in the past, and still is vitally important today.

In the 1950s, it seemed as though the Government of Canada had little input in the Arctic. Apart from some scattered radio and weather stations, their sole representatives were members of the Royal Canadian Mounted Police.

It used to be said (and there was considerable truth in it) that the tiny trading communities and those who depended on them were under the influence of the "big three" — the Church, the Hudson's Bay Company and the RCMP. The HBC did the trading and provided an economic basis for the community; the Church took care of the spiritual lives of the people; and the RCMP acted for the Government. All three certainly looked after the medical needs of the people before nursing stations were established.

In the early days when the HBC had a near monopoly as traders, the "Bay" men, as they were called, considered their jobs a lifelong vocation. Those we knew, along with their families, were profound assets to community life in the settlements. These managers cared for their customers with genuine compassion, but never to the point of providing ready "handouts" or "debt" to individuals showing a lack of initiative or disinterest in trapping. The managers at Coppermine, Manning, Learmonth, Cruickshank, Jones, and people like Bill Munro are still remembered by the hunters and trappers of our generation, most with respect and fondness.

The Bay (as the HBC was referred to) only functioned successfully when trappers brought in furs for trade. I always thought that the trader and the trapper met on equal terms, with benefits for both.

The Church in the North has too often been viewed as an imported institution from the south with all the trappings of a professional business. This is in part true; as an organization, it operates with an infrastructure and accepted practices, with full financial accountability. After all, it is using funds from "Outside", and it is necessary to be accountable for those funds. However, essentially, the Church is really a community of believing Christian people. The day-to-day activities of the Church in the North were (and are) the result of activities of the local missionaries, their families, and their parishioners, including a growing lay ministry.

Its leaders and membership, while inclusive of all northerners, are in the majority made up of aboriginal local people. Worship has consistently been offered in appropriate native languages and dialects. In modern times and recent years, the proclamation of the Gospel remains relatively unchanged. However, addressing the basic spiritual and social needs of each successive generation requires adaptation of methods and focus. For example, in the days we worked in Coppermine, we were never called upon to deal with suicide, substance abuse, teen pregnancy, and other problems that face our clergy today, and alcohol-related problems were just beginning to emerge.

Another major outside influence was the Royal Canadian Mounted Police (always called the RCMP). In our time in the Central Arctic, the police rarely had "police" work to do in the usual understanding of the term, and any arrests or court appearances were uncommon.. "Law enforcement" in the sense of dealing with criminals was generally unnecessary. Their patrols were mainly to see how life in the camps was going on, registering how many animals of each species had been harvested; giving out hunting licenses and making sure game regulations were being observed. They also represented the Government of Canada in the administration of relations with the American military during the construction and operation of the DEW Line.

Relationships with the people were friendly and understanding for the most part. The local policeman dropping into a home for a chat struck fear into no one. The police socialized easily with the people, and the Special Constables who helped them were valued members of their team; indeed most could not have travelled without their help. I have heard that before my time, the word used for "policeman" was *amaguk* (which means "wolf"). However, I have never heard that expression used in all the time I have been in the North.

The North itself, the land and its people, affects people in various ways, and retirement, even for RCMP members, has not always meant escaping to the South. Staff Sergeant Glenn Warner, for example, following many years service in the Mackenzie Delta, Cambridge Bay, and on the DEW Line, has remained in the North. He and his wife, Trish, started an ecotourism lodge at Bathurst Inlet. Now working in partnership with the local Inuit, Glenn Warner's present day "arresting" is by attracting tourists to share in the wonders and beauties of the Arctic.

In those far-off days in the North, the native people were forbidden the use of alcohol despite the fact that these prohibitions were later considered an infringement of their rights as Canadian citizens. However, this prohibition of alcohol did result in communities being practically free of any kind of serious crime. As I recall, in Coppermine, we went about nine years without any cause for a Justice of the Peace to fly in for a court case.

There were problems, of course, but few that could not be handled locally. In all, those days were comparatively idyllic. But however peaceful and acceptable society seemed to be in that era, change was on its way and along a dimension that would radically affect the entire way of life for the vast majority of people.

In the early 1950s, the Canadian Government, as if in anticipation of a later sophisticated defensive radar line, created a volunteer ground force, drawing from the scattered populations across the Arctic. This force was called the Canadian Rangers. Each member was an accomplished hunter, fully at home in frigid conditions and well able to guide and support regular ground troops should a military emergency develop.

I was commissioned as a Lieutenant for the Coppermine Ranger Patrol. My duties included distributing 303 rifles and ammunition to members of the Rangers. These rifles and ammunition could, for practice, be used for hunting, but the real purpose of the Rangers was to serve as Canada's "first line of defence" should an attack be launched over the Pole.

As the 1950s proceeded, world events began to affect the isolated Arctic. First, there was the Cold War, with the Soviet Union clearly identified as the enemy. At the time, the USSR was a powerful nation, located just across the polar ice cap, uncomfortably close to Canada's Arctic region. In the fifties, intercontinental missile systems were in their infancy and not reliable. The main threat to North America was considered to be fleets of manned bombers that could take the cross-polar route to access our continent.

The DEW Line was the result - an impressive string of 58 radar sites located every fifty miles across the Arctic coast from Alaska to Greenland. These were located between the 67th and 69th parallel, north of the Arctic Circle. This was a massive undertaking financed by the US government. All sites were on land, and all were built between 1955 and 1957. The logistics were astounding to those of us living in our isolated little settlements along the coast.

The acronym DEW stands for "Distant Early Warning", but the system name was later changed to "North Warning System". However, across the North, it is still known as the DEW Line, and it changed the North forever.

All equipment and building materials had to be brought in, by air or sea. 140,000 tons of materials were brought in by air; and 281,600 tons by naval sea convoy, plus a lesser amount by river barge and cat train on the sea ice. Because so much cargo needed to be flown in to areas without airstrips, large airstrips often had to be built. It became a military operation, with heavy equipment being flown in by huge transport planes landing on the ice, all done with a sense of urgency similar to that seen in war.

Throughout the construction period, and later for the actual operation of the manned sites, there was a tremendous need for workers. At the height of the construction, more than seven thousand men were employed in the Arctic. Quotas to ensure equal opportunities for employment were non-existent, but this did not mean the local people were overlooked for job opportunities. The military needed workers who were acclimatized to the incredibly harsh conditions in the Arctic, and who knew how to survive and work productively in these conditions. They looked to the people of the North. The Inuit were ideal - a people who had lived for generations on the land, fashioning with their own hands all they needed for survival. They were used to extreme cold and other hardships. This land was their home; they did not pine for the gentle climate of the south. Thus, from hunting camps across the Arctic, men were recruited for DEW Line work. Many were quickly sent out for training as heavy equipment operators or mechanics, careers at which they often excelled.

The construction proceeded apace, and the line was in operation by July of 1957. Many Inuit remained employed during the 30-year operation of the sites. In the early 1960s, the fur market was highly unstable, and income from trapping was uncertain. The highly paid DEW Line jobs were too good an opportunity to miss. Men hired on at the sites, and their families moved to live in close proximity to the radar stations, often settling into "modern" housing with electricity and other amenities. Due to the high quality, reliable, and often exotic (the US military was known for flying in all sorts of wonderful things from fruits to lobster!) food supplied to the sites, people experienced new delicacies, without surrendering their reliance on local game meat.

So it was that an entirely new lifestyle and sets of skills (and an exposure to another new culture, that of the American military) came to the Arctic coast. Some men and their families decided this life was not for them, and soon returned to a simpler lifestyle in which shift work and clock-watching had no place. Others became permanently employed and served for many years at the sites.

About the same time the DEW Line concept was on the drawing board, a small group of people were living completely unaware of all of this, in the vast barrenlands to the west of Hudson Bay. Several groups of Caribou Inuit lived inland along the upper Back River, completely dependent on the caribou migrations, rather like the people of Ennadai Lake described in an earlier chapter.

On Garry Lakes, south of Queen Maude Gulf, a small group of people missed the caribou migrations, and starved to death, much as had happened regularly in ancient times. However, this time, attention of the world was focused on the Arctic, communications were much more efficient, and media attention was further stimulated by the publication of Farley Mowat's two books, *People of the Deer*, and *The Desperate People*. In the latter, he referred to starvations suffered by inland Caribou Inuit in the area to the west of Hudson Bay, about which he had heard.

Mowat's stay with the people he wrote about did not extend to many weeks, but his gift of imaginative writing, a curious blend of truth and fiction, did much to alert the Canadian public to the North and its inhabitants. More importantly, it fueled a groundswell of public sentiment that soon influenced government policies.

Media attention to Inuit starvations also affected the attitude toward Canada on a world scale. In the United Nations, whenever Canada raised its voice about the plight of less fortunate minority populations in other countries, there was an immediate response about Canadian neglect of her own aboriginal people. It became evident that the Federal government had to do something.

In addition, years of mineral exploration that had started in the late 1920s gradually led to an increased appreciation of the wealth that lay beneath the land and waters of the Northwest Territories. By this time, gold mines were well established in the Yellowknife area, adding hard rock mining to the oil production that had been going on in the Norman Wells area since World War II. Oil reserves in the Beaufort Sea were attracting attention, and investment in oil and natural gas held considerable promise.

In the 1960s, a renewed interest in copper in the vicinity of the Coppermine River arose like a phoenix, and claims were staked at a frenetic rate. There was much speculation about the construction of a port facility at Coppermine to allow direct shipment of copper to Japan. Due to high costs of development, no mines were established, but the claim staking led to further exploration.

Shipping attention turned again to the Northwest Passage, and, as technology improved, the transport of materials, especially petroleum, through the Passage became a distinct possibility.

All this attention to the North, added to further developments in nuclear-powered submarines and missile systems, caused the Canadian government immense concerns about its own claim to the Arctic islands. Sovereignty became an issue, and with it came increased attentiveness to the plight of residents of the Arctic.

Consequently, along with an increasing awareness of Canada's northern borders a new sense of obligation on behalf of Canada's aboriginal peoples began to arise. The attention of the government became directed at the people of the Arctic barrenlands.

It is wrong to even suggest that the Government of Canada did nothing for the Northwest Territories prior to the seat of the Territorial Government moving to Yellowknife in 1967. From 1905 to 1951, an appointed Commissioner and a Territorial Council of upper level civil servants governed the NWT from Ottawa. In 1951, three elected Members from the Mackenzie District took their places on this Council, and, between 1955 and 1966, there was a gradual transition from appointed to elected Members. By 1975, the Territorial Government was composed entirely of elected members. It became the "Legislative Assembly of the Northwest Territories" beginning in 1976.

But, from the standpoint of us who lived through the fifties and the sixties in the Arctic, the governmental "presence" seemed to explode at an alarming rate over a very short period of time.

The federal government, determined to avoid the possibility of more starvation camps, and with an eye on heightened security across the North, encouraged camp dwellers to relocate into larger settlements. The attractions were enticing....no more starvation, warmth, housing, and education for children, medical services for all. To people used to living with uncertainty, it all looked very good.

More schools were built in the settlements, and improved as grades were added. Nursing stations were better equipped, and staffed by trained nurse practitioners. Communications improved, and medical emergencies could be handled more efficiently, saving lives particularly of young children. Air service on all-weather airstrips improved; stores like the Northern Stores carried fresh produce.... and junk food. Locally owned Co-op stores made business management a local concern. Recreational complexes appeared, offering all manner of sports. Community diesel generators produced electricity, and suddenly refrigerators and deep freezes, radio, television, and telephones became available. The world had beat a path to the doorstep of the Arctic. People were entranced.

The development of an active mineral industry has been vital to economic development in the Central Arctic. Mineral exploration had continued since the 1920s, waxing and waning with world mineral prices, but became economically important in the 1960s. The North Rankin Nickel Mine opened near Rankin Inlet, employing Inuit who had been moved to a small camp called Itivia on the shore of Rankin Inlet. Inuit employees were vital to the operation of this small mine. Cullaton Lake Gold Mine opened in the interior Keewatin, also providing employment for Inuit. Base metal mines developed on Little Cornwallis Island (Cominco's Polaris Mine), and near Arctic Bay in the northern part of Baffin Island (Breakwater Resources' Nanisivik Mine). Echo Bay Mines started a gold mine on Contwoyto Lake (Lupin Mine), and major exploration projects developed west of Contwoyto and to the east of Bathurst Inlet.

Training and encouragement to young people to stay in school and complete a basic education has resulted in more people being qualified to work in the mining industry.

Then, in the 1990s, diamonds were discovered in the Central Barrenlands south of Kugluktuk and Bathurst Inlet, precipitating a staking rush without precedent in the NWT. The development of two major diamond mines (Ekati and Diavik) has provided additional opportunities for the Kitengmiut and other northern peoples. Thanks to the far-sighted insistence of politicians and strategists, the secondary industries of diamond sorting and cutting/polishing have recently been added to this major groundswell of economic activity. The economic future seems far brighter for Central

Arctic and Great Slave Lake communities.

Along with this growth into modern society, democratic government developed rapidly. This was supported by a growing civil service of educated staff from the local communities, largely the results of higher education. Eventually the Government of the Northwest Territories became a fully elected government, with aboriginal constituents fully represented.

The Inuvialuit Land Claims were settled in 1984, and then, as a result of twenty-some years of work, the Inuit Land Claims were settled in 1993. As mentioned before, the creation of a new territory, Nunavut, was required under the Nunavut Final Agreement. Work continued, this time on the development of a new Territory.

The next major step was "Division", sanctioned by the Government of Canada and the people of Canada, whereby the Northwest Territories divided into the NWT in the west, and Nunavut in the north and east on April 1, 1999.

Several major government initiatives were started to meet the requirements of the settlement of the Inuit land claims, the most urgent of which was that a significant portion of the work force of the Nunavut Government be made up of Inuit. A multitude of courses and intensive training programs has resulted in an increase in the proportion of Inuit employed in the Nunavut Government.

Now, as the new governments struggle with diminishing federal dollars, and increased responsibilities, soaring birth rates, a lack of economic opportunities, and problems delivering acceptable education to a young population, the future is a mixture of serious challenges, though not without hope and optimism.

All these developments took time, of course, but really not much time in the timeless history of a people. Within two generations, the Inuit of the Central Arctic went from a people who knew little beyond their hunting areas to a people who were literally in touch with the world, and to whom Rambo, Pokemon, satellite phones, high-tech fuel injected snowmachines, professional hockey, and email are all now an ordinary part of everyday life. In many cases, people are now far from their cultural past, but there is increasing effort being made to preserve the language, and to connect young people with the elders, to avoid losing touch with the Inuit culture.

Many of these latter developments occurred long after we had left Coppermine for life in Fort Smith, Iqaluit, and later in Yellowknife. However, presenting a picture of the emerging North as it exists today helps in understanding the vast differences between the earlier and simpler days of our time on the Arctic coast compared to life in the North today.

Chapter 32

A Turn of the Page

By the end of the 1960s, we had lived in Coppermine for almost twenty years. The decade of the sixties was certainly a time when vast changes were taking place across the North. Most people had moved in off the land and were living in settlements, which were fast developing in areas where the trading posts or missions had attracted people to camp on a semi-permanent basis. In Coppermine, a diesel generator had long been in operation, supplying electric power for the expanding community. The school and nursing station had both been enlarged. Even our little mission church had undergone several transformations as the congregation grew.

ABOVE: Elizabeth Sperry with son John and daughter Angela.

Fewer families were living on the land away from the settle-ments, and few still used iglus through the winter. In many cases, two-roomed cabins were being built even in the outpost camps. Life once lived in more primitive circumstances was certainly dis-appearing.

My status as a single missionary had changed long before with my marriage to Betty in 1952. She shared (and still shares) my com-mitment to the people of the Arctic coast, which started so long ago. Yet, living in Coppermine, we had a deep sense of isolation, espe-cially when Betty's precarious health necessitated evacuation to the south in a small plane.

One year after our marriage, our hopes for our first child were met with sadness as a little girl, born on March 26th, lived only ten hours before expiring from a lung condition. That experience brought us not only closer to our faith in the provision of our Lord but also gave us a deeper understanding of the sufferings of the people in even worse circumstances, often in isolated camps with no evacuation possible.

I have vivid memories of meeting the arrival of a dogteam in Coppermine, only to be handed a tiny bundle for burial. A weak and weary mother had given birth on the trail only to lose that little life shortly afterwards, all in the most primitive of conditions. Somehow, despite the very different circumstances, the pain of our loss was reflected and understood in theirs. They were deeply sym-pathetic and supportive.

Later we were blessed with the arrival of Angela, in April of 1956, and John, in July of 1959. Both our children, now grown and with families of their own, have constantly affirmed their deep appreci-ation of being brought up sharing in our northern life during those formative years. The love of the country and happy relationships with their friends of those days gave us all a deep sense of appreci-ation, gratitude, and wonder at the joy of sharing life in the Arctic with the people of the land.

For both Angela and John, a deep concern for the developing social problems of their contemporaries led both into careers of social service in the rehabilitation and correctional professions. As a family, there has never once been expressed any word of regret among us about the vocation that took us to the Arctic and contin-ues to bind us to the northland and its people.

A most welcome development, with the passing years, was the steady increase of interest in Arctic missions from the middle fifties onwards. Before 1950, Harold Webster had the care of the Anglican faithful in the entire Central Arctic all by himself. I inherited this area in l952. Happily, by l969, prior to our leaving Coppermine, no less than eight ordained missionaries had joined our ranks, serving in expanding parishes established separately throughout the area.

These missionaries included Donald Whitbread at Spence Bay (now Taloyoak); Gideon Qitsualik at Gjoa Haven; Nigel Wilford at Spence Bay and Holman; William Evans at Cambridge Bay; Peter Emmerson at Cambridge Bay; Berry Capron at Holman; Christopher Williams at Coppermine and Spence Bay; Peter Bishop and Robert Chesterton at Coppermine.

These last four initially spent some time with us at Coppermine for orientation to the culture, and for language study. They worked for varying lengths of time in the Arctic, some moving from our area to the Eastern Arctic later in their lives.

Christopher Williams has offered uninterrupted service in the Arctic, mainly in the east, but now in Yellowknife. He was elected as my successor, the fourth Bishop of the Arctic, prior to Division of the NWT and Nunavut. Peter Bishop succeeded me at Coppermine before becoming Principal of the Arthur Turner Training School at Pangnirtung. He was later appointed Executive Archdeacon of the Arctic. Both Chris Williams and Peter Bishop have served the Diocese for a long period with special distinction.

Two Church Army captains also served during my years as Archdeacon. They were Captains Terry Buckle and Larry Robertson, whose ministries developed in a uniquely tandem fashion. Both served in pastoral ministries, each at Holman and Cambridge Bay at different times. Both were later ordained and elected to the episcopate, Terry as a Suffragan Bishop of the Arctic, then Bishop of Yukon, while Larry was elected regional Bishop of the Western Arctic.

As time went on, both the Federal and Territorial governments played an increasing role in the administration of the North. Government offices were established in regional centres, and increasing interest was shown in the peoples of the North. Following the move of the territorial seat of government of the Northwest Territories from Fort Smith to Yellowknife in 1967, various responsibilities once held by the federal government began to be devolved to the territorial government, and later, to municipal governments.

In Coppermine, the changes were obvious. The Royal Canadian Mounted Police had less preoccupation on maintaining dogteams, and more involvement with law enforcement for the increasing populations in each community.

Two main factors contributed to the need for law enforcement -

the rise in cash opportunities through employment, plus the granting of a franchise for all Canadians, whatever their ethnic background, to consume alcoholic beverages. The impact of these new "privileges", without proper education as to how to live within one's means, generally speaking, had a disastrous effect on settlement life in general and family security in particular. In earlier times, members of the RCMP who had been stationed in the Arctic very much needed a refresher course in the south to get reintroduced to normal law enforcement. By the late 1960s, that day had long passed; they had very real social problems to deal with even in the small communities across the Arctic coast.

Prior to the 1960s, the traders of the Hudson's Bay Company were primarily interested in grading and purchasing fur. In the early days, stores in the Arctic were intentionally unheated, mainly to discourage trappers from hanging around after hurried trading. The traders urged their customers to use the trapping season to the fullest extent possible. The stock carried by the HBC post stores was basic, to say the least; luxury goods were just not needed.

However, once better air transportation systems were developed, the southern department stores discovered a potential northern market, and a new era of consumerism was ushered in. By the 1970s, the Bay stores had tripled in size and offered a wide variety of goods of every description. Suddenly the store interiors were well heated and a rich and varied stock displayed to encourage browsing and the spending of money.

Also, by the 1970s, the silence of the Arctic was shattered forever. Upon my arrival in Coppermine in 1950, there were only three modest outboard engines for boats. Those were owned by the HBC, the RCMP, and the Missions.

Twenty years later, dozens of outboard motors propelled freighter canoes at (to us) fantastic speeds day and night, throughout the open water season. (Today, in an era of jet-boats and 115 hp outboards that fling fiberglass boats through the water at 60 km per hour, the freighter canoes seem incredibly slow.)

And, during the long winter season, the jangle of harnesses and the shouts of dog-drivers have been exchanged for the staccato roar of the snowmobile - dozens of them, speeding around in a manner unimaginable in the fifties. The mournful howls from the doglines, perhaps in response to a wolf call in the silent night, were heard no more. Even the wolves took themselves off to quieter and safer locales.

Urbanization (if we can use that term for a settlement of only a few hundred inhabitants) had a distinct effect on community life as

a whole. This was particularly obvious for the young people, especially following the years after we left the Arctic coast. Increasing
influences from the south and the alluring and exciting images
relayed by television signals and videos offered the watchers and
listeners options of a decidedly unhealthy nature. The social fabric
of Arctic society was beginning to fray, presenting some very dis-
turbing developments.

Chapter 33

Mission Impossible?

In many parts of the world, history has recorded the profound effects of life in urban or city communities, often in sharp contrast with life in rural and wilderness areas. The contrast is often more obvious in regard to attitude toward religious beliefs and practices. Religious beliefs are often taken much more seriously in areas where people live close to the land. The Arctic experience well illustrates the truth of this. The first proclamation of the Gospel of Jesus Christ to a people who lived in constant fear of malignant spirits, controlled by taboos and the threat of shamanistic curses, was received as very good news indeed.

During the years of my ministry, almost everyone had accepted

ABOVE: Prayer was truly part of the life of the people.
Kituligak, Ida Aivak, Ruth Nigiyonak in a tent at Naloayuk.

the Christian faith, taking part in public worship at every opportunity. I can recall days on the trail when travellers would not take a drink of tea or munch on a hardtack biscuit before offering a prayer of thanks. With no visible source of help in that vast wilderness, without medical services, social relief or emergency food supplies, all were dependent upon their own skills and ingenuity, and upon Providence.

It was simply accepted that it was the Lord who provided them with food, and it was accepted that their survival and well being depended also on their God. Many might indeed classify that kind of acceptance of the Christian faith as "folk religion" - an exchange of uncertain animalistic ideas for a more favourable understanding of a divine creative source. Be that as it may, as in all so-called Christian societies, the degree of personal conviction and commitment of faith varies enormously.

So would the faith experienced in the isolated camps - evinced when the Lord of the wilderness was regarded as an "ever-present help" - be subjected to a crucial test when all manner of new and alluring entertainment options became available.

Notwithstanding, even as the resident population in Coppermine steadily grew, church attendance required three extensions of the building to hold all the people. It took only the ringing of the bell quickly to fill the church. But, it has to be said; at that time there were very few competing distractions. Without recreational centres, TV, bingos and more, there was little else for people to do, and they gravitated naturally to the Church, which provided fellowship and comfort.

Year-by-year, an increase of support agencies, particularly in the medical and social assistance fields, became a part of settlement life. These affected the sense of security even to the point of transferring some of the earlier belief in and dependence on divine assistance to dependence on a benevolent government. There were only a few signs of this trend during the latter years of our Coppermine ministry; but far more were on the horizon.

Urbanization had an increasing effect on community life. It definitely affected the younger generation, which would experience little of the careful upbringing, wisdom and culture of their parents and grandparents. There were a few exceptions but not many.

The increasing influence from the south played a large part in this process. Communication through radio, television and videos of every description, were beamed into the poorest of homes. These images and messages presented options of ethics, morals, and lifestyles often in marked contradiction to accepted standards in even moderately Christian societies.

Together with collapse of the fur markets for fox pelts and seal-skins, gainful employment became a serious problem for everyone. The malaise of youth, though not unknown throughout the rest of the country, seemed particularly serious in the aboriginal communities of the North. Dysfunctional families, family and spousal abuse, alcohol and drug dependence, together with frightful numbers of suicides, tragically became the stuff of which northern life was characterized. Sometimes this was unfair, often discounting the witness of worthy and upstanding Christian families who certainly had not disappeared.

Slowly, it became obvious that there was a small core of people for whom a sincere and genuine Christian faith was a reality. For others, church attendance became a Christmas and Easter pilgrimage with casual appearances for weddings and funerals. It was obvious that the Church, which proclaimed the power and presence of God in the wilderness, was facing the challenge of speaking to the needs of people in a very different context. If the Christian Gospel has any authenticity at all, with the love and power of almighty God being demonstrable in all human situations....then it is the Church's mission to communicate the same by witness and tangible ministry in understandable terms. That is, and always has been, the task of the Church.

The modern missionaries, in my opinion, have a far more demanding and exacting task than had their forebears. Rightfully, we herald the pioneers; Edmund Peck of Arctic Quebec and Baffin Island; Bishop Bompas, the pioneer for the northwest, and others. They suffered incredible hardships and great physical duress for the Gospel.

We of a later generation, with less privation, also undertook long dogteam journeys, leaving our families for weeks. But, despite it all, all the mental stresses of a later generation were unknown and unimagined. Throughout the early years of our service, there were comparatively few social problems. Alcohol-related problems were almost nonexistent. Teenagers were too busy learning the skills of their parents to sink into apathy. Small wonder that the missionaries of our generation were required to serve for a period of five years in the Arctic without a furlough. Indeed, "stress-related burnout" had no place in our vocabulary.

The modern missionary enters a scene that still has many of the challenges of the earlier period, including an understanding of the culture and the need to learn the local dialect in order to minister to the people in their "heart" language, especially for the elders. These days, the clergy may not have to pull teeth or deliver babies but, almost daily, their ministry involves counselling people suffering marriage breakdowns, spousal, elder or child abuse, or chronic depression. They may need to attend court sessions, talk to parents about delinquent children, or deal with suicide attempts, and so on.

All the strains and stresses of a good pastor or priest in any of our southern situations are compounded and laid upon the shoulders of today's Arctic missionary. They may not spend their time merrily driving dogteams or conducting weddings in snowhouses, but they need a double portion of the spirit of the pioneers and must be of equal stature in zeal, faith, and caliber as those of the past. They, too, have been set aside and tasked with the sharing of a Gospel, which needs to be declared in the power of the Holy Spirit.

On the positive side, as the years have gone by, the Diocese of the Arctic has witnessed some very clear evidences of God's grace and power among His northern people, stewardship in both giving and service. Committed Inuit Christians have offered to dedicate their lives to the Church and have been accepted for the ordained ministry, gifts to God from their own culture. Their knowledge and understanding of their own people is superb, learned in a manner outsiders can only gain at great cost. As the new Millennium dawned, the indigenous leadership of the Diocese includes Paul Idlout and Andrew Atagotaluk, both from North Baffin, who have been ordained as regional bishops to assist Bishop Christopher Williams in the Eastern Arctic area of the Diocese.

Despite all the troubles and complexities of this modern era, the age-old message of healing and renewal in the name of Jesus Christ is proving as valid for this generation as it did for those Arctic iglu dwellers who so gladly accepted the same Gospel those many years ago.

What a privilege it has been to have such a share in that proclamation!

ABOVE: *Dogteam*

Epilogue

Having acted as editor for *Igloo Dwellers,* I feel it is appropriate to bring readers up to date on the Sperry's lives following their departure from Coppermine.

From Coppermine, the family moved to Fort Smith, south of Great Slave Lake, where Jack was appointed rector of St. John's Anglican Church for the following four years.

Jack was able to continue translation work, enjoyed gardening during the summer months, and even played tennis with son John and friends. Betty offered her services at St. Anne's Hospital and took a position at the local health centre. During these years, Angela continued her education at Balmoral Hall, an Anglican boarding school in Winnipeg, Manitoba. John attended Joseph Burr Tyrrell School in Fort Smith.

In 1974, shortly after being appointed as rector of Holy Trinity Anglican Church in Yellowknife, Sperry was elected the third Bishop of The Arctic. The Sperrys spent the following two years in Iqaluit, prior to moving back to Yellowknife. During this time, the Diocese of The Arctic, which for a few years had been divided, east from west, once more united into one.

As time passed, both Angela and John attended Camrose Lutheran College, in Alberta. Here, Angela met her husband-to-be, Douglas Friesen. During the following years, living in Yellowknife, they have had two children, Andrew and Catherine.

John met and married Kathy McCollum, daughter of family friends, Archdeacon Turq and Joan McCollum of Hay River. Presently, John and Kathy live in Hay River, where they have two little girls, Olivia and Elizabeth.

Since retirement in 1990, Jack has continued a busy ministry as an honorary associate at Holy Trinity Church. He is also a chaplain at the Canadian Forces Northern Headquarters in Yellowknife, for the Royal Canadian Legion, and for the Stanton Regional Hospital. Previously, he retired from a voluntary ministry for the Canadian Bible Society as National President, besides being a Vice-President for the United Bible Society Americas Region. These positions have required travel to a number of countries.

In her characteristic unassuming fashion, Betty has continued an equally important parallel ministry in the life of the Parish with special emphasis as a seasoned counsellor, always available for the careworn and distressed.

In the summers, Bishop Sperry is also involved as a resource person and field instructor for Bathurst Inlet Lodge, located in the tiny community of Bathurst Inlet, one of the stops on his long dogteam journeys from Coppermine.

It was at Bathurst that I met Jack Sperry, and have continued to work with him each summer. Together with the Warner family, the Kapolak and Akoluk families and other Kingaunmiut, we offer a way for outsiders to learn about the Arctic and the Inuit culture. Jack's role in this endeavour is profound, in addition to helping operate the lodge's large boat, he shares stories and photos with approximately one hundred guests each summer. In addition, he continues to minister to the Kitengmiut, offering regular church services and officiating at weddings, christenings and funerals.

The Warners and the Kingaunmiut of Bathurst Inlet join me in saying that Jack Sperry's presence in our lives has meant the world to us. He has helped all of us through rough times, and his cheerfulness adds sparkle to our time in an astounding land.

It has been an honour to be able to assist you in telling this story, Jack.

Kuanakutin.

Glossary

Unless otherwise explained, all Inuktitut terms are in the Inuinaktun dialect.

Adliak: Sled used by the Copper Inuit, consisting of two long runners and a series of crosspieces lashed across the runners. Originally pulled by dogs or humans, now pulled by snowmobiles.

Aglektun: Taboos, customs which, if followed, conveyed protection from evil spirits.

Agiuktun: In Inuinaktun, term for group of powerful evil spirits resembling bags of blood, invisible to ordinary people but visible to a shaman.

Amaguk: Wolf.

Angakuk: Shaman, spiritual leader of pre-Contact Inuit groups.

Atigi: Parka or jacket, usually made of caribou skin with the hair on the inside. Also a term used for any outer parka that does not have the caribou hair on the outside.

Aiyungnangman: "It can't be helped." Expression deflecting any need for control of a situation.

Break-up: In the Arctic, time when rivers and lakes are losing their ice cover due to warm weather in springtime.

Canadian Eskimo Dog: Internationally recognized name for the aboriginal dog that accompanied the Inuit across the Bering Land Bridge.

Candle ice: Ice that, in springtime, splits along long lines of vertically-aligned crystals, about the size and shape of candles.

Chipewyan: The most easterly group of the Dene tribes, with home territory in northern Manitoba and Saskatchewan, northwest almost to Great Bear Lake.

Conibear trap: Modern quick-kill traps made of heavy steel bars that crush an animal's chest or break its neck.

Copper Eskimo/Inuit: Anthropological term for the people living in an area in the Central Arctic, Victoria Island south onto the central part of the mainland Arctic coast, from west of the Coppermine River east past Bathurst Inlet to east of the Perry River.

Dene: Generally used term for the aboriginal people of the southern part of the central NWT, south of the treeline, between the Mackenzie River and the east end of Great Slave Lake. Includes the groups of people known as the Dogribs, the Yellowknives, and Slavey.

Diocese of The Arctic: Ecclesiastical area which in the 1950s covered some 1.5 million square miles, from the western boundary of the NWT east to include all of Arctic Quebec.

Division: Term for all activities leading to the political division of the Northwest Territories into the Northwest Territories and Nunavut.

Dorset: Inuit group reaching prominence from 1000 BC to 1100 AD, spreading from the Foxe Basin are across the Arctic. Probably did not have dogs, and likely invented the snowhouse.

Eskimo: Indian (probably from an Algonquian source) word meaning "eaters of raw meat", formerly used for the indigenous people of the Canadian Arctic who developed from the Eskimoid groups.

Eskimoid: Anthropological term for all the peoples of the Arctic coast, from Alaska to Greenland, referring to a group of people with linguistic and physiological affinities.

Falla: Inuinaktun term for a priest, "Father".

Fan hitch: Dogteam hitch arrangement whereby each dog is attached by a long line to the front of the sled. Used most frequently in the eastern arctic where teams must negotiate jumbled shore ice.

Freeze-up: In the Arctic, time during the fall in which lakes and rivers are freezing; term for the development of a cover of ice on all bodies of water.

Frostbite: Freezing of various layers of the skin due to low temperatures and (often) wind.

"The Great Commission": Command recorded in Matthew 28:19: "Go and make disciples of all nations." This has been responsible for the development of evangelical movements throughout the history of Christianity.

Hunianik: A curse, placed on a person.

Iglu: Or, ***igloo*** (Eastern Arctic use, which has become accepted as a term all over the world). Snowhouse, house made of blocks of snow stacked in a spiral fashion, top closed with a key block, and spaces chinked with snow.

Ikaluakpak: Huge fish. (Inuinaktun.)

Inlanders: People who spent most of the year to the south of the coast, living on the inland lakes, hunting caribou and fishing.

Inuinait: People who live along the central Arctic coast, in the Inuinaktun dialect.

Inuit: Name for people of Eskimoid origin now living in the Canadian Arctic.

Inuk: Singular of Inuit; indicates one person.

Inuktitut: Name for the language spoken in the eastern Canadian Arctic.

Inuktitut syllabics: Inuktitut language in written form expressed in symbols that represent certain sounds.

Inukshuk: Stone figures on the land to guide people or mark something. Local Inuinaktun term: ***inukhuk***. Plural: ***inuksuit*** or ***inukhuit***.

Inumagiktut: Eastern arctic term, meaning "truly people".

Inupiat: Name for aboriginal people living along the Alaskan arctic coast.

Inuvialuit: Name for people, originally from Alaska, who now inhabit the Mackenzie Delta and parts of Victoria Island plus the arctic coast east past Paulatuk.

Inuyuk: "He or she lives", referring to people alive today.

Kakivak: Leister or fish spear with central barbed point and two side pieces that helped to grasp the fish.

Kamik: Inuinaktun term for skin boot, common footwear in the winter.

Kavlunak; kavlunait: Singular and plural for "white people", or essentially non-Inuit. Also: ***kablunak***.

Kavlunaktun: Or, ***Kavlunaaqtun*** (Inuktitut). The English language.

Kayak: Or, ***qayaq*** (Inuktitut). Skin-covered small boat, used mostly for hunting caribou at crossing places.

Kila: Rolled up fur clothing in a bundle, sometimes used for divination of answers to questions posed by a shaman.

Kinmit: Dog, sled dog.

Kitengmiut: "People of the Middle"; general term used for the Copper Inuit, people living in the middle part of the Arctic coast.

Kuak: Frozen fish or caribou, which is eaten by slicing off thin strips. It is highly nutritious and tasty.

Kuana: Thank you.

Kuanakutin: You are a cause for thanks. (Thanks in a more formal fashion.)

Kudlik: Or, qulliq (Inuktitut). Soapstone lamp used for cooking, light, heating in a snowhouse.

Kugluktuk: Present name for the community at the mouth of the Coppermine River, formerly known as Coppermine. In Inuinaktun, means "rapids" or "falls".

Kulitak: Outer parka or jacket, usually of caribou skin with the hair on the outside. (Inuinaktun)

Kuviahugvik: "Time of happiness" (Inuinaktun), usually referring to the Christmas season. Eastern arctic variation: ***Quviahugvik.***

Leghold trap: Steel traps made to grasp the leg of an animal when sprung. These were fastened down with a chain so the animal could not drag the trap away.

Lemming: Small mouselike rodent with a short tail.

Maniilak: Rough ice, such as might occur in a pressure ridge.

Minihitak: Minister, clergy. Plural: ***minihitait.***

Mipku: Dried meat, usually caribou, a staple of the diet of the Kitengmiut. Also: mikku (eastern arctic version).

Mug-up: Break from travelling in which tea is consumed, along with pilot biscuits or whatever happens to be handy.

Naguguta or naguaguta: "Helping familiar spirits" which assisted a shaman.

Nome hitch: Arrangement of dogs on a team, side-by-side, attached to a central gangline.

Northwest Territories: Former name for all lands east of the Yukon boundary and north of the 60th Parallel. Now refers to lands east of the Yukon and west of the Nunavut boundary, which was set based on traditional use of the barrenlands, "within living memory." The NWT, Yukon, and Nunavut are all Canadian "territories", as opposed to provinces; there is more federal control.

Nuglugak: Traditional game in which a bone piece is strung between floor and ceiling, and twisted and released. Players attempt to get a pointed spear through a single hole in the piece of bone or antler.

Nunamiut: People of the land, referring to the Inuit and Inuinait of the Arctic.

Nunavummiut: People who live in Nunavut. (More recent use.)

Nunavik: Current name for the area formerly called Arctic Quebec, still part of the Province of Quebec.

Nunavut: New territory formed by the division of the NWT into western and eastern territories, Inuit homeland, Canada's newest territory. Means "our land" in Inuktitut.

Paleo-Eskimo: Groups of people who migrated across the Bering Land Bridge from Siberia to Canada some 5,000 years ago.

Pektuk: "Blow" or blizzard.

Pipfi: Air-dried fish, used as a staple food in the Central Arctic. Not smoked, just dried by hanging in the open air and wind.

Principle of dynamic equivalence: Concept that the inner meaning of a text must be expressed in a way that makes sense to the people who will be using it (as opposed to a translation forced upon them).

Pualuk: Mitts. Plural is **pualuit.**

Punchy snow: Term used for snow when the temperature rises to just below freezing, and the snow becomes soft and water saturated. This creates difficult travelling conditions.

Qangmak: Snowblock shelter like half an iglu, roof is often a tarp or caribou skins. This spelling is the eastern arctic spelling, because this refers to shelter used in starvation times, in the Kivalliq region.

Roman orthography: Inuinaktun and other dialects of the "Eskimoid" language expressed phonetically in letters familiar to all who read English or other western languages.

Shaman, shamans: General term for people who apparently had magical powers and were in touch with the spirits. Shamans could perform acts of magic and were believed to be able to heal or harm by magical means.

Shiptime: Term used to refer to the arrival and unloading of supply vessels across the North.

Skraellings: Norse term for Inuit.

Talu: Stone hunting blind or "hide", which enabled hunters to get close to caribou.

Thule: Whale-hunting culture migrating in from Alaska and the Bering Straits about 800 AD, and occupying most of the Arctic by the 1500s. During the "Little Ice Age", (1650 – 1850 AD), they changed their culture to depend less on the large whales and more on smaller sea mammals and caribou. They became the modern Inuit.

Tingmiak: Airplane. Literal translation is "bird".

Treeline: Transition zone between coniferous forest and tundra, a ragged and indistinct line extending from the Mackenzie Delta southeast to Churchill on Hudson Bay.

Tupilak, tupilait: General term for evil spirit. *Tupilait* is plural, more than one evil spirit.

Ukiuk: General term for both "winter" and for "year".

Umiak: Large boat used for transport of families and worldly goods on the sea. These were usually made of a frame of wood upon which a walrus-skin covering is attached.

Umialik: "Boat-owner"; person who has primary responsibility for the boat.

Upatitkatik: "Sharers of the flippers", close friends or hunting partners who would traditionally share parts of a ringed seal.

Suffixes:

- hiuk: (Used in the middle of a word.) Seeking or looking for.

- miut: People of.

- tut: "Like" or "similar to"

Some words for snow:

Snow is obviously a big part of life in the Arctic. There are many words for *"snow"* in Inuinaktun. These are just a sample:

Apiyuk: snow covered

Apun: snow on the ground

Auvik: snowblock

Igluhak: snow for building an iglu

Kanek: falling snow

Mahak: melting snow

Mingulik: powdery snow

Patukun: sparkling snow

Pukak: sugary snow

A short language lesson:

Words in Inuinaktun can form whole thoughts, with various suffixes (formerly "affixes") strung together according to a set of rules too complex to explore here! An example of the Inuinaktun word for the phrase: "I will make you searchers for people."

Inukhiuktinguktitauniaktuhi

This word breaks down this way:

Inuk	**hiuk**	**tinguk**	**titau**	**niak**	**tuhi**
person	looking for	to become	to be made	will	you all

Bibliography

The following titles are suggested for further reading for wider coverage of northern life and history. Some are out of print. If any of these volumes cannot be found in public libraries, they may sometimes be found in used bookstores or through a search service.

Bruemmer, F. 1971. **Seasons of the Eskimo; a Vanishing Way of Life.** McClelland & Stewart Ltd., Toronto.

Burt, P. 2000. **Barrenland Beauties, Showy Plants of the Canadian Arctic.** Outcrop, The Northern Publisher. Yellowknife, NT.

Crowe, K. 1974. **A History of the Original Peoples of Northern Canada.** Arctic Institute of North America/McGill-Queen's University Press, Montreal. 226 pp.

Teabreak on the trail. Sam Oliktoak and Sperry.

Davis, R.C. 1995. **Sir John Franklin's Journals and Correspondence: the First Arctic Land Expedition, 1819-1822.** The Champlain Society and the Royal Canadian Geographical Society, Toronto and Ottawa.

DeCoccola, R. and King, P. 1989. **The Incredible Eskimo.** Hancock House, Surrey, BC. 435 pp.

De Poncins, G. 1941. **Kabloona.** Reynal & Hitchcock, New York. 339 p.

Eber, D. H. 1989. **When the Whalers Were Up North.** Inuit Memories from the Eastern Arctic. David R. Godine, Boston. 187 pp.

Fleming, A.L. 1956. **Archibald the Arctic, the Flying Bishop.** Appleton-Century-Crofts, Inc., New York.

Gordon, R.G. 1996. **The North Copper Inuit.** University of Toronto Press, Toronto, ON.

Gunn, Anne 2000. Notes from program delivered at Prince of Wales Northern Heritage Centre on the biological effects of global warming, particularly on caribou.

Hall, Ed. (Ed.) 1989. **People and Caribou in the Northwest Territories.** Dept. of Renewable Resources, Govt. of the NWT, Yellowknife, NT.

Harrington, R. (Edited by Edmund Carpenter) 2000. **Padlei Diary, 1950.** Rock Foundation. 110 pp.

Harrington, R. 1981. **The Inuit; Life as it Was.** Hurtig Press, Edmonton.

Houston, C.S. (Ed.) 1984. **Arctic Ordeal; The Journal of John Richardson, Surgeon-Naturalist with Franklin, 1820 – 1822.** McGill-Queen's University Press, Montreal.

Houston, C. S. (Ed.) 1974. **To the Arctic by Canoe; The Journal and Paintings of Robert Hood, Midshipman with Franklin.** McGill-Queen's University Press, Montreal.

Houston, C.S. (Ed.) 1994. **Arctic Artist; The Journal and Paintings of George Back, Midshipman with Franklin, 1819-1822.** McGill-Queen's University Press, Montreal.

Hunt, W.R. 1986. **Stef, A biography of Vilhjalmur Stefansson.** University of British Columbia Press, Vancouver, BC.

Jenness, D. 1922. **Life of the Copper Eskimos, Vol. XII.** Report of the Canadian Arctic Expedition, 1913-1918. Southern Party. F.A. Ackland, Ottawa.

Jenness, D. 1928 (1992 reprint). **The People of the Twilight.** University of Chicago Press, Chicago.

Jenness, D. 1946. **Material Culture of the Copper Eskimos, Vol. XVI.** Report of the Canadian Arctic Expedition, 1913-1918. Southern Party. F.A. Ackland, Ottawa.

Jenness, S.E. (Ed.) 1991. **Arctic Odyssey; the Diary of Diamond Jenness, Ethnologist with the Canadian Arctic Expedition in Northern Alaska and Canada, 1913-1916.** Canadian Museum of Civilization. Hull, PQ.

Mallory, E. 1989. **Coppermine; the Far North of George M. Douglas.** Broadview Press.

Marsh, D. B. (Edited by Winifred Marsh) 1987. **Echoes from a Frozen Land.** Hurtig Publishers, Edmonton.

McGhee, R. 1978. **Canadian Arctic Prehistory.** National Museum of Man, National Museums of Canada, Van Nostrand Reinhold Ltd., Toronto.

McGhee, R. 1996. **Ancient People of the Arctic.** UBC Press, Vancouver, BC.

Morrison, D. and Germain, Georges-Hebert. 1995. **Inuit, Glimpses of an Arctic Past.** Canadian Museum of Civilization, Hull, PQ.

Mowat, F. 1958. (Reprint 1990) **Coppermine Journey.** McClelland & Stewart, Toronto, ON.

Moyles, R.G. 1979. **British Law and Arctic Men.** The Celebrated 1917 Murder Trials of Sinnisiak and Uluksuk, First Inuit Tried Under White Man's Law. Western Producer Prairie Books, Saskatoon, SK. 93 pp.

Oakes, J. 1991. **Copper and Caribou Inuit Skin Clothing Production.** Canadina Ethnology Service, Mercury Series Paper No. 118, Canadian Musuem of Civilization, Hull, PQ.

Pielou, E.C. 1994. **A Naturalist's Guide to the Arctic.** University of Chicago Press, Chicago, IL.

Rasmussen, K. 1927 (1999 reprint). **Across Arctic America, Narrative of the Fifth Thule Expedition.** University of Alaska Press, Fairbanks, Alaska.

Rousseliere, Guy Mary. 1991. **Qitdlarssuaq; Story of a Polar Migration.** Wuerz Publishing Ltd.

Sperry, J.R. (Translator) 1972. **Gospellit Hitamat Apostellit Havangillu** (Gospels and Acts) Canadian Bible Society, Toronto.

Sperry, J.R. (Translator) 1992. **Atutit, Kengautillu (Inuinaktun/Copper-Eskimo) [Atugnaktun Anglikamiuni] Book of Common Prayer & Hymns.** Diocese of The Arctic, Anglican Church of Canada.

Tester, F.J. and Kulchyski, P. 1994. **Tammarniit (Mistakes): Inuit Relocation in the Eastern Arctic, 1939 – 1963.** UBC Press, Vancouver.

Wilson, R. 1989. **Thank God and Dr. Cass.** Outcrop Ltd., The Northern Publishers, Yellowknife, NT.

Index